Affiliate Marketing:

Develop an Online Business Empire by Selling Other People's Products

Adam Wolf

Table of Contents

Introduction

With the advent of the Internet, people have been exposed to a wide variety of things. Working/earning from home has been one of the most important advantages of this technology. Affiliate marketing has been taking the world by storm on this front. With innovations in coding and technology, interactive web pages and cookie trackers are now capable of predicting which products you are most likely to buy. This is the reason you find advertisements magically materializing when you are in the midst of researching something online.

Most of us would have shied away from purchasing those items but the pop-up advertisements give us tempting deals and offers. When a person clicks on that advertisement, he has already made sure that somewhere in the world someone was able to cash in. That is basically what affiliate marketing has to offer. It is a bridge that works both ways; benefitting both the parties involved, i.e., the business concerned and the webmaster.

It is precisely this double benefit model that keeps

everyone hooked. In this pattern, there are no losers, only profits for everyone. The webmaster does not have to shell out any cash to jump onto the affiliate market bandwagon and the business owner is not obliged to pay anyone until he makes a sale. So in such a potential win- win situation for all, what prevents everyone in the world from becoming a part of it? What kind of money do the people involved stand to earn? What are the secrets to a successful career?

This book aims to enlighten you about the way affiliate marketing works and how to become good at it. It also showcases some of the finer details and explains why one should be wary while treading into the field. It is my hope that upon reading this book, you will be able to successfully start an affiliate business of your own with the knowledge needed to thrive in the field and overcome the most common obstacles that affiliate marketers usually have troubles with overcoming. I want to thank you for choosing this book and I sincerely hope you find it informative.

Chapter 1

What is Affiliate Marketing?

Affiliate marketing is a type of marketing in which one is rewarded for every customer brought in by the affiliate's own marketing efforts. Affiliate marketing is usually considered an industry with four major players: The merchant, the network, the publisher and the customer. The merchant is also known as the retailer or the brand; the network is where the affiliate chooses the offer and it also deals with the payments. The publisher is also known as the affiliate and the customer is the one who finally buys the product. This affiliate marketing has grown complex over the years and it has resulted in a secondary level of players derived from the affiliate marketing field, such as super-affiliates, affiliate management firms, and third-party vendors. The affiliate system has two sides in the actual world of marketing: the advertiser and the producer/merchant.

The definition of affiliate marketing, according to marketer and blogger Neil Patel, is "the process of spreading product creation and product marketing across different parties, where each party receives a share of the revenue, according to their contribution." It isn't just one or the other; neither merely advertising nor merely creating the product.

It doesn't matter which you are, the publisher or the producer. You can be either and make a profit.

We already know what the components of an affiliate marketing structure are. Let us take a detailed look at these components now.

The Merchant: Other names for the merchant are the producer, the brand, the vendor, the seller, or the retailer. The merchant is the one who makes whatever is being sold. On one end of the spectrum you could have a major organization, such as Samsung, which produces microwaves, among other things.

On the other end, you could have one person, such as Mariah Coz. She creates and sells courses online targeted at women who are or want to become businesspersons.

Anyone can be a trader starting up a system with affiliate marketing, right from an individual business person to a Fortune 500 company to a startup. They don't need to be effectively included; they simply need to have an item to offer.

The Affiliate: Another name for someone in this group is publisher. Affiliates can also range from single people to whole organizations. The marketing takes place here. What an affiliate does is to advertise one or more items to draw in and persuade potential buyers that the vendor's item will have potential value to convince buyers to purchase the item.

One of the ways this is accomplished is by running a blog that reviews the vendor's products. Another way to do this could be to create a website, the sole purpose of which is to find and promote products that are considered "cool" and are focused on one particular topic.

The Consumer: The entire affiliate framework works because of the presence of the consumer or the customer. Without the customer's purchases, no commissions can be earned and no income can be divided up.

The affiliate generally uses whatever channel they think is appropriate to promote the product to the customer. It could be through a blog that utilizes content marketing, social media, or even digital billboards.

Whether the purchaser realizes that he or she is involved in a framework to do with affiliate marketing depends upon the affiliate.

There are those who let their buyers know and a lot of affiliates have a tendency to be straightforward about the fact that their marketing is manipulated monetarily; however, there are those who don't.

In the case of the latter, tracking software runs behind the scene. In this case, the customer goes about making purchases as per normal. The affiliate gets a percentage on every purchase that the customer makes.

Network: Not all definitions consider the network a working component of the system of affiliate marketing. Having said that, the role a network plays is that of a go-between for the merchant and the affiliate.

Nothing stops you from marketing a course online that someone else has designed and created and directly sharing the income with them. However, giving a network a chance to handle the installment and item conveyance lends a more genuine to your attempts at affiliate marketing.

There are instances when affiliates have no choice but to involve a network just so they can market a product. For instance, this situation could arise if the product has just been released by the vendor on the network and nowhere else.

As such, the network becomes a sort of log or database for a lot of items and products. The affiliate may decide which product he or she would like to promote.

If you are thinking about marketing consumer products such as toys, tools, household items and books, the largest such network you will find is Amazon. You have the opportunity to market anything that is up for sale on Amazon's platform, thanks to the Amazon Associates program. There are no restrictions on who can join and Amazon allows anyone to create customized links to products on Amazon. If somebody buys anything by clicking on your link, a small percentage or commission is paid to you.

Now that the fundamental terms have been elucidated, how about we get a general idea of how to best plunge into affiliate marketing?

What Is the Best Way to Proceed?

As I mentioned earlier, there are fundamentally two sides to an affiliate marketing system.

You can become a dealer and get others to advertise your

item, in return for them receiving a percentage from the sales made by them.

Then again, you can become an affiliate who promotes one or a few items that you'd get a kick out of the chance to elevate and showcase to shoppers, keeping in mind that the end goal is to profit.

While the vast majority begins by going via the affiliate course and it is unquestionably the less demanding way to take, putting together enough movement to make an important salary only from affiliate deals isn't speedy or simple.

That is the reason I'll show you the four essential steps that are needed to begin regardless of which side you choose

Four Steps to Becoming a Merchant

If you want to be a dealer and afterward profit by getting affiliates to offer your item, you will need to follow four basic steps. While these steps are basic, they aren't exactly easy, so pay attention.

To begin with, you need an idea for a product. I'll demonstrate to you some methods by which you can produce those thoughts, based on what's well known as of now, in the following segment.

Second, you need to make sure that your idea is a good one. Of course, you could start working on your project idea straight away. However, you may want to consider the possibility that people don't need it. Products can only be profitable for you if they are needed.

Third, you need to follow through on the idea and make the product. Because fashioning a physical product carries with it all sorts of risks and requires a fairly large investment, we'll talk about making online products. You are advised to begin with these, since they require practically no cash, only your time.

In addition, once you have created your product and put it out there, you're not done. Affiliates who will market your product still need to be found.

Here we go!

1: Thinking up of an idea for a product

Most people believe that thinking of an idea is the difficult part. That's not true. Coming up with ideas is actually quite simple.

However, if you are under the impression that the idea should come only from your own brain and must be the most original thing ever thought of, then you could be in trouble.

If the goal is to profit through affiliate marketing, you don't want to become sentimental about your idea.

You're better off thinking long and hard about what services and products are already available on the market. Consider how they can be enhanced by conveying something that takes care of the issues with those items.

You can, obviously and dependably, pick a subject that you're intrigued or engrossed in.

Envision that you're a stay-at-home Dad or a housewife, for a brief moment.

Possibly you need to make an item that makes family unit tasks less demanding. For instance, you could look at a vacuum robot and think up of a few ideas.

The first result upon doing a Google search is a site that reviews robot vacuums.

Great!

Just by taking a gander at each of the reviews, you can observe what's not so great about these robots and what could possibly be enhanced.

The robot doesn't have virtual walls. These could determine where it should clean and where it shouldn't. This problem seems to be fairly common with six reviews out of ten mentioning it – and this just in the top products!

No remote control is likewise a typical "con."

Notwithstanding, the virtual wall was mentioned over and over again.

Subsequently, a good idea you could consider is to build up a virtual wall that functions regardless of which vacuum robot is used.

If you are able to create a system that gives the robot vacuum a virtual wall, you could interest anyone who actually owns one of those things. Your system could allow the robot to clean only a space that has been predetermined.

Don't you think that is a significant idea?

I'll demonstrate to you that it can work for anything.

Another means you have of conducting research is a device known as Buzzsumo, which demonstrates to you what's prevalent, in terms of social shares.

If you want to build sandcastles, the first thing to do would be to search for what content is popular right now. This is something that can be done instantly.

On the off chance that you search YouTube and look for "construct a sandcastle," you'll discover a huge number of results.

Clearly, individuals truly need to learn how to assemble cool sandcastles. All in all, what would you be able to do?

Create a progression of recordings where you demonstrate to individuals well-ordered and generally accepted methods for assembling five particular epic sandcastles.

Then again, you can conduct a review of the majority of the devices that you have to manufacture brilliant sandcastles.

Another thing you can do is to think of a few stencils or structures that individuals can use so that making cool sandcastles is a heck of a lot simpler.

The question arises: Will individuals be ready to spend money on it?

2: Verify your idea

Keeping in mind that the end goal is not to do an awesome arrangement of sandcastle recordings that nobody needs, you need first to test your thought.

How would you do that?

It's quite easy: You ask individuals to purchase it from you.

How would you discover these individuals? Simple.

Find the sandcastle posts that are listed on Buzzsumo and copy one of the URLs. Then connect it to a device known as Topsy.

Topsy demonstrates to you a rundown of the greater part of the general population who posted that link on their Twitter feed.

Then you can specifically educate them regarding your thought, by clicking on the reply option.

Make sure that you find out whether they'd be willing to pay for your idea, not just whether they like the idea.

People will mention that an idea is likeable, because they want to be pleasant.

If they say yes, you have to specifically follow up with a request that they purchase.

Remember, saying that they'll pay for it and actually paying for it are two different things.

At the point when individuals are intrigued by your item, allow them to purchase. You can use PayPal and tell them that you're going to construct it if you receive a specific number of requests.

You can begin making the item when you cross the limit you set and know that individuals really need it.

3: Creating the item

Depending upon the product or service you've decided to create, there can be many steps to creating the item. While this isn't a handbook on entrepreneurship, here are some ways you can start.

As I mentioned earlier, physical products can require a lot of cash and time. Since I want to ensure that those resources aren't wasted, I'm going to focus on helping you create a digital product.

Online courses

Ebooks

Podcast/Audio

These are great beginning stages. It's much easier to make digital products, since they really only require your time and maybe some amount of money. That money generally takes the form of a fee for a service or the price of a piece of software.

When you have created the item and sent it to the people who are going to buy it from you initially, you can set about organizing the affiliate network.

4: Finding affiliate accomplices

The easy thing here is the tech part.

With instruments such as Digital Product Delivery or Gumroad, you can, without much of a stretch, set up partnerships with affiliates and permit them to gather commissions.

The hard part is discovering affiliates who really have a crowd of people who are keen on what you offer.

We should continue with the sandcastle control illustration.

Do you believe there's anybody there who offers something even distantly connected?

Really, there is.

When you Google "figure out how to manufacture sandcastles," a few sites appear that offer instructive material about it, such as Sandcastle Lessons and Sand Sculpt USA, both of which offer lessons on building sandcastles.

Reaching them and inspiring them to collaborate on a deal together would be a simple pitch, since it's an immaculate fit.

The more specific your item is, the less demanding it will be to pitch to kindred merchants.

You can essentially send them an email, present yourself and the item, and inquire as to whether they want to work out an income-sharing deal together.

Genius tip: Commissions of half or higher are exceptionally basic with advanced items, since you have no cost of replication. Try not to be insatiable here; split the pot equally and everybody wins.

Googling "toy survey blog" likewise gives a lot of results where individuals review toys.

Also, some YouTube channels review particular classes of toys. On the off chance that you discover one that surveys children's toys, they'd presumably additionally be a solid match.

Simply have a go at discovering one individual to partner with and begin your first affiliate advancement. You can change commissions and subtle elements later; the vital part is to begin.

Be that as it may, you could likewise begin the adventure on the opposite side of the fence and simply turn into an affiliate yourself.

Four Steps to Becoming an Affiliate on the Web

As with becoming a vendor, there are likewise four steps that you can take to begin your trip as an affiliate advertiser.

First, you have to begin assessing items in your specialty. That should be possible on a YouTube channel, on a blog, or even simply utilizing live streams on Periscope.

Second, you need to gather messages, so you can associate with your group of onlookers whenever you need and don't need to seek after them to see your substance.

Third, you can utilize joint wander online courses to make a considerable measure of offers in a brief timeframe, while at the same time developing your email list and making new substance.

Finally, once your affiliate business begins profiting, you can scale your development with pay-per-click promoting.

1: Review items in your specialty

It's less demanding to begin as an affiliate, since you're skirting the "have a thought" portion of becoming a vendor.

You already utilize and like a lot of items, so all that you need to do to begin is to discuss them freely.

Begin by taking a gander at the accomplices in Step 4 for becoming a vendor, since that is what you're attempting to begin in this progression.

Any item works.

Truly.

Investigate this person, who surveys Hot Wheels tracks and autos.

More than 300,000 endorsers for Hot Wheels? I'm certain that, whatever your specialty is, it's less particular.

In the event that you like reading, survey books:

Take note: An uncommon sort of review that generally does truly well is the correlation with an immediate contender.

You'll soon discover a lot of individuals who are already doing this. Simply scan for "best hair straighteners," and observe.

This blog surveys level irons for straightening hair (for women). How specific of a blog is that?

She can identify with the item, as she needs to straighten her own particular hair. What's more, in the event that she does her exploration well, the blog is well positioned in Google, and it really helps women to locate the most ideally equipped instrument for the occupation.

Whatever you're evaluating, make sure that you do likewise.

On the off chance that your surveys aren't really useful, individuals will detect, instantly, that you're simply attempting to make a brisk buck.

As Pat Flynn points out, included affiliate marketing is by a long shot the most beneficial, on the grounds that you can really identify with the item, rather than simply advancing something that may make you a great deal of money.

When you don't know the item, how would you be able to promote it soundly?

Take note: This is somewhat more specific to shopper items than it is for online courses or books made by people. In the event that you've known a man for quite a while and believe them and know their work is awesome, that is a different thing.

When you write reviews on your blog, you can utilize affiliate connections to connect to the items that you advance.

You can remember them on different online journals by the long "/ref..." tail, toward the end of the standard connection.

This is generally the initial step to begin making commissions.

Just join Amazon Associates and you can then continue to get your own particular affiliate connection to any item on Amazon.

Simply go to the item page and tap on "Short connection to this page." You'll get a connection that will give you a commission if individuals buy through it.

Nonetheless, on the off chance that you just depend on individuals using the affiliate interfaces as a part of your surveys, it implies that you require loads of movement to really begin profiting.

However, in the event that you figure out how to contact your group of onlookers straightforwardly, you can market to them at whatever point you like, not only when they are visiting your site.

This is the place step 2 comes in.

2: Build an email list with your prospects on it

Email is still one of the best marketing channels today, so you don't want to give it a miss.

Here are three methods you can use to get your visitors' email addresses; they are all very simple to use.

Number 1: Hello Bar

You can put a call-to-action on the top of your website using a "hello bar." This bar is visible to anyone who visits your website.

In the call-to-action, you can offer visitors various incentives to enter their email address. For example, you could offer them a free e-book for signing up.

Once they click on the call-to-action or hello bar, it will

send them to a page where they can enter their email address and receive their free gift.

Number 2: Exit Gate

Hello bar can also be used to create an exit gate. When visitors are about to click out of your website, an exit gate creates a pop-up than prompts them to enter their email address.

Generally an exit gate is triggered when a visitor moves his or her mouse moving to the top area of the browser.

Another way to get email addresses from your visitors is to redirect them to your lead magnet and then do this.

Number 3: Sidebar Widget

You will find many blogs that have completely cluttered up sidebars.

Don't repeat their mistake.

Too many choices can confuse your visitors. Chances are that they won't click on anything at all.

It's best to have only one call-to-action in your sidebar. Like the hello bar, it too should offer a gift or incentive in return for your visitors' email address.

Remember that you'll be collecting email addresses for topics revolving around very specific things, such as microwaves, building sandcastles, and so forth. Therefore, you won't need too many email addresses to make this work.

Even if fewer than, say, 500 people sign up, you can still generate a significant number of sales.

Make sure that you send those who've signed up regular updates, preferably once a week. This keeps them engaged and coming back for more.

It shouldn't be just about sales. Let them know whenever you post a new review.

From time to time, send them a definite call-to-action. It could be a review for a new product that you've tried and found worthwhile.

You can tell your visitors that you have something new and great, why you feel that way about the product, and why you think and recommend that they shift to this product.

But that's not all. Once your email list consists of at least a few contacts, this is what you can do.

3: Educate your gathering of people with live online classes

Online classes are marvelous.

Suppose that you need to purchase another microwave.

What makes you want to purchase an microwave more:

Reading a review on a blog?

Seeing a live presentation of a microwave in real life?

Number 2, obviously!

Using something like LeadPages, you can create a landing page where visitors can agree to take your online class.

Promote your online class via web-based networking media for a week ahead of time and inspire individuals to join.

At that point, you can, without much of a stretch, host a Google home base, which is totally free, to stream your online course live to your gathering of people.

An online class is an awesome way to draw in your group of onlookers one on one to demonstrate the item that you're promoting and answer any inquiries that they may have.

You can:

- exhibit the item's components

- indicate diverse utilize instances of the item

- discuss its advantages and downsides

- tell individuals your own history with the item

- help your group of onlookers receive the most in return

- and much more.

Tip: Learning how to have an online course with a Google Hangout takes under 10 minutes.

Imagine how enthusiastic your crowd will be when they see the cool things that your product will empower them to do.

Indicating your affiliate connection and sharing it near the end of the online course is an excellent offer and easily falls into place, since you spent an hour discussing the item.

It won't feel forced and your buyers can take the time that they need to decide on whether they'll really buy.

Professional tip: Can you get your dealer to give you an exceptional arrangement for your gathering of people? If you guarantee to get their item before a few hundred individuals, they'll frequently cheerfully give you a rebate or uncommon package to facilitate manipulate individuals to purchase. With this technique, you have a good chance to get your audience to purchase your item.

They have an opportunity to purchase after the autoresponder arrangement, on the online class and from future messages.

At the point when your business begin rolling in and starts to develop, that is when you can truly explode your business with paid promotion by simply directing people to business instruments that work.

Internet marketing methods overlap affiliate marketing to some degree because regular advertising methods are used by the affiliate; that includes SEO (search engine optimization), e-mail marketing, paid search engine marketing, content marketing, and also displaying advertisements on banners, which is very common these days. Affiliates also use some other less orthodox techniques, such as reviews of the product or services offered by a partner.

Difference between Referral and Affiliate
Referral marketing is commonly confused with affiliate

marketing because they both use third parties to drive sales to the retailer. However, they are very distinct, different forms of marketing. The main difference is that trust and personal relationship are paramount to driving sales in referral marketing, whereas affiliate marketing relies p u r e l y on financial motivation to drive sales. Advertisers usually overlook affiliate marketing. While search engines, website syndication, and electronic mail are used to attract and capture t h e attention of the vendors, affiliate marketing has a lower profile than they do. Still, a significant role is played by the affiliates in an e-retailer's marketing strategies.

Inception of Affiliate Marketing

The concept of affiliate marketing was brought to the Internet by William J. Tobin in 1989. Affiliate marketing has grown very quickly since its inception. The e-commerce website, which in the early days was thought of as a marketing toy, later became a more integral part of the overall business plan than the offline business that was already in existence. Sectors such as gambling, retail industries, and file- sharing services became the most active sectors of affiliate marketing. Several affiliate solution providers anticipate a hike in interest from the B2B marketers and also a rise in the number of advertisers using affiliate marketing as part of their mix.

Later Internet developments, such as blogging and interactive online communities, have helped to improve communication between affiliates and merchants. Web 2.0 also started many new online business platforms to improve and enhance the quality of communication between the merchants and the affiliates. Affiliate marketing is very popularly known as "performance marketing," a reference to how sales employees are typically being compensated. Advertisers don't employ the affiliates. Affiliates are usually known as the extended sales arm for the business that is very often used to describe affiliate marketing. Network program managers and affiliate managers are used to run outsourced program management companies that are being used by the merchants. The roles of an advertising agency server and the affiliate program management performed by the OPM companies are similar.

Chapter 2

Brief History

Affiliate marketing is basically a type of performance-based marketing, where people who influence others are rewarded by retailers for every new customer acquired through the marketing efforts of the influencer. Affiliate marketing has changed very much over the years, i.e. before Internet and after Internet. The birth of the Internet made things easy for the retailers and the customers.

The concept of affiliate marketing has changed much since the World Wide Web came into existence. For instance, an example of offline affiliate marketing is when a hairdresser offers you a discount for referring a friend of yours. However, this was considered a very old method and the tracking was difficult because tracking of referrals should be done in such a way that it allows the affiliate to be paid, which was a difficult task. The rise of the Internet not only helped in advertisement but also helped in revolutionizing almost everything.

People started looking on the Internet for information, reviews, and recommendations before buying products and these became a key element in a brand's marketing strategies. Technological developments like the advent of Web 2.0 and the introduction of cookies created a method for tracking the impact of advertising on the purchase funnel. With the big entry of ecommerce in the end of 1990s, blogging in the early 2000s, and content developed by the users soon after, the field was set for affiliate marketing. Affiliate marketing was patented by William J. Tobin. He set up the first affiliate marketing program for PC Flowers and Gifts, his very own company, in 1989.

Amazon was one of the foremost companies to use affiliate marketing with the introduction of its associates program in 1996. This attracted many people from all over the world and was widely considered, as the model retailers needed the most. Commission Junction and ClickBank were two affiliate companies that were launched in July 1998. The launch of these two companies made the network of affiliate marketing a lot more accessible to online retailers smaller than Amazon. This was achieved by offering solutions for payment and facilitating exchanges between affiliates and the merchant. Very soon in 2000, the Federal Trade Commission of the United States introduced guidelines for the sector, which helped in making affiliate networks cement their legitimacy in the online marketing world. In the same year, Amazon declared that it had been granted a patent on components of the programs of affiliate.

Whenever visitors clicked on the website to purchase a book, the associate would receive a commission. Though it was not the first merchant website to offer an affiliate program, the model of Amazon became very popular and served as a model for the subsequent programs. The patent application that was submitted by Amazon in June 1997 predated most of the affiliate programs.

After nearly eight years, in 2008, more legislation was introduced across the US to further enhance and regulate the field. Since its inception, affiliate marketing has grown very quickly. The big secret of the Internet is that adult sites started coming up with many of the best concepts in market that was used in the mainstream. The UK's Internet Advertising Bureau offers even more insight into the practice.

Chapter 3

Why Affiliate Marketing Is Good For You

There are many reasons that could encourage one to be a part of affiliate marketing.

Portable and Convenient

Nowadays, affiliate marketing is done through the Internet. This makes it very convenient and profitable. Your job suddenly becomes a whole lot more flexible than before and you have the chance to make any place your workplace. This increases your efficiency without compromising on your daily life.

Affiliate marketing is a portable, global and flexible job. Because it is an online job, it is portable. You will be able to work anywhere in the world, provided there is an Internet connection available. With the advent of Wi-Fi technology and it being free in most public spaces, it is easier to see why it is flexible and portable. You can get a new affiliate, keep track of current projects and enjoy your coffee at the same place and the same time. If you are traveling, there will be waiting time that you can exploit to do affiliate marketing and be productive. Since there is no set working time limit or a punch card system to track your time throughout the company, you do not have to worry about being on time. You can work twenty-four hours a day, seven days a week if needed. Moreover, your income does not stop just because you have switched off your laptop. The website will continue to operate and you will still earn.

A Part-Time Profession

Affiliate marketing can also be done as a part- time job that will give you a little extra cash while you stay at home. This is called a passive income. Anyone can do affiliate marketing: For example, a student who wants to earn a little extra during college to pay off tuition or a retiree who wants a little extra along with his pension. It does not cost anything; you will simply sign up with a company to allow them to post their advertisements on your blog or website.

Low Investment, High Return

If you think of affiliate marketing as starting up your own company, then you can see that the startup cost and overhead is very low. With a regular business, you will have to consider getting a loan, finding a place to set up your company, and worry about sales and overhead. All of this worry goes away in affiliate marketing; you do not need a ton of money to start the business, you don't have to worry about rent for the company and there is no worry about staff payments and taxes.

This is similar to billboards: The billboard owners pay money to the building owners to advertise on their building. The payout from this method of advertising is far greater than the costs incurred. There is no need to worry, as the advertisement companies will be paying you as long as the advertisements are on your site. On top of all this, you are the sole proprietor for the business and you have to pay nothing to run the company.

Your job is simple; you have to put the links the company gives to you on your blog or website and wait. You have to wait for a customer to click on the link. You will get the commission as the salesman and you have done nothing physically to try to sell the product. You save on energy, time, and effort that you can invest in your day job, or other things that are more productive. This is helpful for bloggers; they can spend their time writing great content rather than worrying about making ends meet.

Minimal Office Management

Having no staff or building to take care of means that administration is minimal. You don't have to persuade customers to push your products, do not have to worry about sales to pay your staff, and, more important, you do not have to worry about the customers returning things. The only thing you have to do is make sure your readers click on the advertisements. That can be achieved by using advertisements that are related to the website or blog that you are running.

The Freedom of Choice

The main advantage of affiliate marketing is that you can choose your affiliations. You have the freedom to choose what you want to advertise. There is no one to stop you from doing the things you want to. No one is going to force you to advertise a particular company. On top of that, if you advertise the same things your blog or website is about, it gives your viewers a place to start. They will click on the advertisements to start for themselves. Let's say your website is about gardening. You affiliate with a well-known gardening retailer; this opens up the opportunities for you and your viewers to purchase. You can push products by reviewing them, by recommending them and sharing personal experience using the products. You have to be careful not to over-sell the product, which may raise red flags about the review.

When you have just started out with the affiliate marketing idea, don't just sign up for the first advertisement you see. Think about which advertisements will suit your website. Be on the lookout for cheaters; they will ask you to put many advertisements on your website and will not pay you for those on time, or even never at all. Don't be afraid to pass up companies, as many companies are willing to pay for advertising their product. When you promote the companies you are comfortable with, you also increase the loyalty. The most important thing is not to advertise things that are not related to your website. This will make the readers think that you are forcing the product down their throat.

The Sky Is the Limit

An important thing to note about affiliate marketing is that there is no limit to how much you can make. Some people run small affiliate marketing businesses from the comfort of their homes, while others run huge online companies making millions of dollars.

The expression "The sky is the limit" can be applied to the affiliate marketing business; there are few other

businesses in which the potential for growth is so huge. You could start your business today with a small blog or website and a few years from now, with enough work and dedication, you could be running dozens if not hundreds of specialized blogs or authority websites. You could be selling all sorts of products that fit your niche.

You also don't have to limit yourself to just one market. You can have several businesses in different niches to test different markets and strategies to find one that works. You are only limited by your imagination and the time you are willing to put into this. With a little time, some hard work and effective strategies you can have several different businesses that can generate passive income.

Chapter 4

Benefits

With affiliate marketing, a merchant is able to gain more customers through well-placed advertisements on the website. This saves time that the merchant can spend on more useful things. It also allows the merchant to gain access to a larger stage on which sell his product when compared to conventional advertising methods like television, radio advertisements, and billboards. This also means that the merchant need not search for the customer; instead, the customer comes to the merchant.

Data at a Glance

The merchant can compile a statistical database of customers through the affiliate's site. This gives the merchant a reliable behavior analysis of the customers. The marketing system gives the website an additional income source. Small websites that have just started will find it useful, as it gives them a financial foothold to run the business. The financial gain of the affiliates is also increased, as there is minimal investment on their part. This system is based on the fact that the merchant does not have to pay the affiliate until the visitor becomes a customer. Furthermore, the business owner does not have to pay unless his product is sold. Generally, there is a minimum amount that has to be sold before the business owner has to pay.

This benefits the customer, as the affiliate's site goes to the delivery part as well. The customer does not have to physically move to get the product; rather the product is delivered to the customer directly. With the increasing dependency on search engines every day, the affiliate can make sure the merchant is listed higher in the results. This improvers the chance of the customer going to the link for the merchant and increases the opportunities gained by the merchant. Another advantage of search engines is that the advertisement does not have a down time. Most of the times, the membership scheme gives the affiliate's website the choice of merchants to advertise to the customer. By knowing their audiences, the affiliates can sell more of a specific product and ensure that the customer does not leave the website quickly and unsatisfied. Most of the time, the affiliate's website will have campaigns to target specific types of people to buy certain types of product. This brings in permanent customers and the ability to sell a targeted product to consumers.

Marketing; Part of the Package

The affiliate will take care of the marketing for the merchant. The affiliate makes sure that the merchant comes to the top of the search results in important search engines. This is particularly important for small businesses that have just started and are looking for a foothold. This strategy gives rise to a new demand. The merchant need not wait for the potential customer; instead, the potential customer finds the merchant. The customers create demand and the merchant's sales increase. The affiliate increases the chances of the merchant being found by using multiple listings of the merchant in the search engines. The real competition is to get into the top two result pages of the search engine. This gives the merchant the highest chance of being found.

More Transparency Equals More Trust

A major financial advantage that affiliate marketing gives to the merchant and the affiliate website is that the sales are transparent. The money can be tracked and the location of sales can be found very easily. This helps if there is any discrepancy in the sales. Most merchants run their companies with minimal hardware and investment. It is the fastest home-based company to start. There is no financial risk in affiliate marketing, as there are no limitations to earning in affiliate marketing. You also have a live count of the number of audiences that are visiting through the merchant's site. This also tracks the number of products sold and the profit you have made.

You are Your Own CEO

Since affiliate marketing needs no big investment in infrastructure, you are your own boss. You can work when you want and where you want. You can adjust your timing to deal with your customers and different timings to deal with the merchants. Being your own boss, you have the ability to choose the merchant sites that you want to promote and the projects that best suit your interest. This helps you to maintain maximum concentration and does not make you resent your job. Another perk of starting the business from home is that you can work from any place you like. If you are moving to a new location, there is no need for you to shift the entire company. You can continue working, as your company will mostly be contained on a laptop or a personal computer. It is easy for you to shift your location of work without worrying about losing your clients. This also means that you will have job opportunities everywhere. You might lose some of your clients, but there will be new clients who will need your help.

Every Day Is a Holiday

Travelling to different countries for a vacation puts you into a positive feedback loop that ultimately benefits you. When you visit these countries, you learn about their cultures and you are able to advertise better to these countries. This not only gives you the time to relax but also the time to improve yourself and to learn the culture.

Unlike working in a corporate office, you do not have to worry about end-of-month expenses and running out of cash when the month is ending. When you are working through affiliate marketing, if you are successful, there is no limit to your earnings. The cash flow is virtually endless. Affiliate marketing lets you develop your skills. In a corporate setting, you do not have lots of scope to develop yourself, as your boss or senior will be limiting your growth. In affiliate marketing, you don't have a boss; you are your own boss. You can develop your skills as you do affiliate marketing and have free time to relax.

When you make affiliate marketing your full-time job, you can take breaks, travel and take your job with you. As there is no specific location for you to work, you can virtually take an endless vacation and work at the same time. You can do what you love and live your life to the fullest. You can earn during your vacation and enjoy it at the same time. If you are doing affiliate marketing as a part-time job to earn a little bit extra, you can try out your hidden talents and learn new things.

Since both the merchant and the affiliate get incentives from affiliate marketing, it is a really great means of advertising. For the last two years, this has been a field that is growing by leaps and bounds. This is because a lot of webmasters have come to the realization that online advertising can be handled most efficaciously using this method. It is greatly adaptable and gives various advantages that aren't available with other advertisement programs. Here are some:

Low Entry Price – When you start out setting up an affiliate system, it won't break the bank. Startups often don't have the kind of money that most marketing strategies or online ads require, since the startup is focusing on using its money to provide good services and products. When it comes to affiliate marketing, you should simply have your site up and buy an affiliate arrangement; no other expenses are incurred before your promotions begin paying off.

No Staff Means You Save Money - An affiliate arrangement permits you to abstain from hiring a sales staff that needs to be paid by making it your affiliates' responsibility to generate sales. You'll create savings that could go into setting up your business in different ways, and you don't have to make payments unless there are sales.

Just Pay Once the Promotions Work - The most critical piece of the affiliate marketing scheme that you create is that you won't ever have to pay for advertisements that don't generate any revenue. This is because your affiliates profit only when they convey quality activity.

Additional Traffic for Nothing - The advertisements your affiliates put on their websites will generate traffic; however, just a segment of that activity will bring about deals. Therefore, you get extra site hits for nothing, a reward in addition to the deals your affiliates are generating for you.

Better Page Ranks because of Inbound Links – Most search engines rate inbound connections exceedingly when it comes to page rank. Therefore, building up a system of publicists connecting to your website expands your rank. What's more, in light of the fact that your promoters will probably be in a similar field, the relevancy of their website can help to boost the rank of your page all the more.

Control Is in Your Hands - Your affiliate plan is completely dictated by you, permitting you to decide the rates of commission, figure out what allows your promoters to be paid, and for the most part control each component of your publicizing framework. If you want to get all that you can out of the marketing program, this is absolutely vital.

It Simply Works – The affiliate program you create has one last advantage; once you have set it up, nothing needs to be done other than selecting some new affiliates and sitting tight for the sales to start. The product will give your content, different ads, and banners to affiliates. It will also consequently record effective deals. It can even compile invoices for the commissions. All you need to do is send payments to your affiliates and the framework will run as long as you need it to.

Without a doubt, any promoting technique brings with it a

few dangers. Notwithstanding, risking these money-related dangers is the shrewd decision that helps you achieve clients without extraordinary misfortune. You don't need to sidestep advances in technology that will permit you to influence the force of a completely coordinated affiliate program. If you are a brilliant entrepreneur, you can step into sales driven by affiliates that will increase your odds of online efficiency.

A suitable affiliate marketing system allows your business to improve, thanks to a framework that reduces the affiliates' learning curve. Indeed, beginning with an affiliate plan ought to be an even move into effective publicizing.

Why utilize an affiliate plan rather than other publicizing techniques?

Affiliate marketing gives anybody hoping to begin or already operating a business online the adaptability and power to expand very fast and the ability to make the essential deals that get the business started up. It is financially savvy and guarantees you won't squander your financial plan on costly projects that don't bring purchasers. Also, you create associations with affiliates who are helpful for you, as they all run well-trafficked sites

It is crucial to build a network of affiliates once you get started; it permits you to continue developing, and will give you the added advantage of developing your rank on Google. If you have many sites directing traffic your way, you're going to offer significantly more than you would if you do nothing but pay for text links. Best of all, since you have no startup costs and no recurring costs that don't have anything to do with sales, the affiliates you network with come at a bargain price!

Chapter 5

Choosing Your Niche

So you know what affiliate marketing is and how it works in principle, but the question remains: What are you going to sell? Deciding on this is the single most important decision you will have to make. It will dictate the course of all the decisions you will be making going further.

The particular direction in which you intend to take your online business is called a niche, and there are many factors to consider when choosing your niche. Looking at the basics, you will want to choose a niche, if possible, for which you already have a certain affinity. Although this is not always necessary, it is a good place to start. Furthermore, you will want to choose one where the competition is not so fierce, yet one that people are actually interested in. Finally, you will want your niche to be fairly valuable if possible, as certain niches tend to attract more customers with deep pockets willing to purchase, while others often attract recreational Internet users who are just browsing and do not intend to use the Internet to buy products.

When it comes to finding a niche with low competition and reasonable value in 2016, be prepared for a challenge. The reason for this is the fact that so many people have gone into affiliate marketing looking for an easy way to make some money, and many of them have made a success from their affiliate businesses. This is why most good value niches are already well covered and the competition is strong within them. Beating the competition in a highly competitive niche may require lots of time, money, and effort. All of which a beginner affiliate may not have in abundance.

Looking into smaller niches that are less covered may be the right idea for you when looking to start up an affiliate business. There are new things hitting the market every day and finding a niche where affiliates have not yet completely saturated the market will often give you great results. You will be able to rank higher on Google with your posts, reach customers before other affiliates have reached them, and generally start making money sooner rather than later. This is the final goal, after all.

There is nothing wrong with starting in a small niche and

expanding into a bigger one once your business grows and your websites start making you passive income, or you make enough money to reinvest. Once there is more money in play, you may want to try and take on some of the bigger players in some of the more covered niches with the intent to try and overtake them and make yourself a big player in a big industry. Naturally, ranking well for certain types of products that are searched by millions will make you more money than ranking well for a specialized product only a handful of people need, but it will also be much more difficult to achieve that ranking.

Ultimately, choosing a niche will come down to research. You will want to research the Internet well, by looking at various niches, starting with the ones you already have an affinity for. If you are an expert in a certain field, you may want to choose that niche despite a strong competition as there may be much you can bring to the niche. Otherwise, simply try to find a niche that has a relatively high value and relatively little competition, and where you believe you will be able to make a breakthrough into the market in a reasonable fashion.

The last thing to remember when choosing the niche for your affiliate business is not to be discouraged if you fail the first time. You may need time to stumble upon the niche that fits your talents and that you can make money from. So, don't be afraid of failure, just keep moving forward and remember that success is not achieved overnight. Affiliate marketing is certainly a business where a lot of money stands to be made and becoming an expert in it will pay off greatly with time.

What Pays Well?

Not every product is the same to sell via affiliate programs. Affiliate commissions range from 1% to over 50% on some products or services and, when choosing your niche, one of the crucial factors to know will be what kind of commissions you can make by selling the products in your niche. The most favorable products to sell are usually electronic products, such as E-books or subscriptions to various online services, as these products will often pay over 50% of the overall price tag.

Various products on Amazon, for instance, start at 4% and selling a big number of products per month can take the number up to 8.5%, which is a huge difference. However, in order to increase your Amazon commissions, you will need to sell hundreds or thousands of products so don't let that affect you too much when choosing what kind of products you want to start selling.

In the end, there is no reason not to change your niche or add other niches to your portfolio when the time is right and your business has grown. For starters, you will likely be best off choosing a niche and type of product that will earn you high commissions, as this will be the easier way of making quick money.

You shouldn't pick a specialty just because you like it. Try not to misunderstand me; enjoying your specialty is something worth being thankful for, but you also need to know it will make a profit for you.

The exact opposite thing you need is to invest a considerable measure of energy and exertion building an affiliate site, only to find that there aren't numerous beneficial items you can promote.

So that is the place you ought to begin: Find a specialty that is brimming with beneficial items, so you know it's conceivable to profit there.

The best items to promote as an affiliate are generally computerized offerings; for example, ebooks or web-based preparing programs. They frequently pay you 50-75 percent of the deal, which you just couldn't do with physical items like apparel or toys.

That is the reason we're going to search for beneficial specialties in ClickBank: It's one of the biggest affiliate networks loaded with advanced items, it's anything but difficult to explore, and you can utilize the "gravity" channel to see which ones are offering admirably and which aren't.

You can take a gander at physical stock down the line on the off chance that you need to, yet for the time being we're simply hoping to see which themes have a decent spread of items that offer.

1: Check out the Categories in the ClickBank Marketplace

When you reach the ClickBank commercial center, you'll see that there are a many general classes recorded down the left-hand-side.

Clickbank Categories

On the off chance that you tap on any of these classifications, you'll see considerably more subcategories you can investigate.

Since there is such a variety of alternatives, it pays to

simply begin with something that looks fascinating. All things considered, the more intrigued you are, the more inspired you'll be to take every necessary step.

For my case, I'm going to take a gander at "Eating regimens and Weight Loss" in the "Wellbeing and Fitness" specialty.

Clickbank Subcategory

2: Filter out Products that Aren't Selling

As of now, I can see 396 items in the "Eating regimens and Weight Loss" subcategory:

That is a ton of items! Also, not every one of them will be beneficial high-dealers, so it's a great opportunity to eliminate the excess.

Set the base gravity to 6 to expel items that aren't offering admirably.

Instantly, this has removed 333 items that aren't offering. I'm left with 63 beneficial items in this subcategory.

This insider tip is obtained from AffiloBlueprint, which is our driving affiliate marketing instructional class. You can look at it to get considerably more nitty-gritty specialty explore procedures.

A few classifications will have a considerable number of items with a gravity of at least 6, and some will have none, by any stretch of the imagination. So if the specialty you're taking a gander at doesn't have any choices, after you apply the gravity channel, simply continue looking around.

3: Browse the Site to Find the Best Niche Options

From here, you need to chase through the commercial center to discover a theme that has a better than average number of items with a gravity of at least 6.

This isn't generally as clear as simply experiencing the sub-classes in ClickBank. For example, you may find that there are many items identified with "detox," but they're scattered over a few unique classifications.

So you'll likely spend a short time burrowing through the classes and searching for subjects that appear consistently. A decent approach to discover comparative items that may show up in various classifications is to utilize the inquiry box at the top.

If I'm perusing in "Eating methodologies and Weight Loss," for instance, and I consider a so-called detox item that is supposed to burn fat...

Detox Affiliate Product

...I may want to do a search for "detox" to get an idea of how many different items like this there are with a gravity of at least 6. For this situation, there are 23.

Look for Detox

This is the reason it's smart to use the inquiry feature once in a while: I would not have discovered these items by looking in any one class or subcategory. I can think about a couple subcategories where detox items may appear, but the pursuit permits me to see every one of them on the double.

Now, I'm thinking that "detox" resembles a promising specialty since it has a great deal of items that are now have admirable offerings. It's unmistakably a specialty that individuals are purchasing.

In the event that you run a search and there are fewer than 10 items with the 6+ gravity, it may be best to pass and search for something else. This doesn't imply that the specialty would be difficult to profit with, but it would probably be harder than a specialty with bunches of items that are offering great payouts.

4: Dig a Little Deeper; Check Out the Sales Pages

Before I decide that detox is the niche I want to consider, I need to take a gander at the business pages for these items to ensure that I have effectively comprehended what the specialty point is, and that the vast majority of the items are on-subject with that.

The top item in my hunt, for instance, is a "PC detox" item, which doesn't fit with my unique thought of "detox eating less" by any stretch of the imagination:

Detox My Mac

Gratefully however, on the front page of my search I can see 7 items that are applicable to the "detox eating less" specialty I'd expected, similar to this one:

21-Day Sugar Detox

A considerable number of them look very expert, and I realize that what they're offering is all around ok, so now I feel genuinely certain about the detox specialty.

It May Take a Little While to Find What You Want

Not all specialty research will be as fast and smooth as my case, which was for the most part an instance of "here's one

I arranged before."

You may run over a couple of dead end before you find an incredible specialty thought. Try not to be disheartened! Simply make yourself some tea or espresso or hot cocoa, and give yourself some an opportunity to glance around and think.

Various Things to Consider before Choosing a Niche

After you've done the process described above and settled on your choice in view of the information, odds are you've found yourself a decent specialty. In any case, there are some additional things you might need to consider before securing it:

A) Is this Niche "Evergreen"?

It's vital to contemplate internally, "Are these sorts of items certain to be well known?"

Some things such as the iPhone released last season will be on offer a lot sooner than any requests drop off. Obama '08 bumper stickers may have been enormous dealers in 2008, but they unquestionably wouldn't be now...

Likewise, a few items may be popular now, yet their

notoriety may be occasional. The Halloween ensemble specialty, for instance, is just going to work during the couple of weeks paving the way to Halloween itself.

To make affiliate marketing worth your while, you truly need something that will be gainful year-round for a long time to come.

You can more often than not make an informed guess just by applying some rationale, but if you need certainly, take a stab at running your specialty through Google Trends. For instance, if I enter "detox" and set it to show results from the previous 12 months, I can see that it's had reliable interest year-round with a January spike (presumably because of New Year's resolutions).

If I change my inquiry to cover the previous couple of years, I can see that interest has been consistently developing, which is likewise an extraordinary sign.

B) Are People Looking for this Topic in Search Engines?

Something else you might need to consider before settling on a specialty is: How many individuals are looking for this topic in Google?

It's incredible if many individuals are looking for your

specialty point in Google for several reasons: It demonstrates that the specialty is sought after, and it implies it'll be simpler to utilize SEO (search engine optimization) to get visitors to your site.

It's entirely simple to check how many individuals are looking for a theme in Google as well: Simply go to AffiloTools (free access for Affilorama individuals).

Once you're in AffiloTools, explore to the watchword inquire about module.

Search for extremely wide and bland expressions identified with your specialty thought. Utilizing my "detox" case from earlier, I'd enter phrases like "detox," "detox eating regimen," and "detox wash down."

In the results, I can promptly observe that there are a few terms getting more than 1,000 month-to-month looks, which is an awesome sign.

If you can discover no fewer than 10 phrases with no less than 1,000 month-to-month searches this way, think of it as confirmation that there's solid enthusiasm for the specialty, and you'll have the capacity to utilize SEO down the line to get movement to your site.

C) Do You Like this Niche?

A final thing to consider before settling on a specialty is: Do you like it? I know I said before that loving a specialty isn't sufficient — it likewise must be beneficial — and that is valid. Be that as it may, it's less demanding if you do like your theme, also.

In the event that your specialty completely exhausts your brains out, or you disliked it for reasons unknown, you'll require the inspiration of Andy Dufresne in *The Shawshank Redemption* to complete your site. (For the individuals who don't have any idea what I'm talking about, the character dug his way out of jail with more than 17 years of work with a stone mallet.)

The man was driven, yet it doesn't need to be that difficult for you. You can pick a specialty you like.

Having in any event some enthusiasm for your specialty will likewise make it less demanding for you to understand your future visitors, which will be useful when you're attempting to showcase your site and your items.

So, if you're taking a gander at a specialty you've concocted, and you truly would prefer not to proceed with it, take a stab at looking again to check whether there's something you'd like more. There will dependably be more than one alternative.

Choosing among Niches

By now, you ought to have a general specialty chosen, for example, "detox eating routine" or "training a puppy," with a modest bunch of applicable ClickBank items that have a gravity score of at least 6.

In the event that you don't have the above, then you have to keep running back through this lesson, picking an alternate specialty and items. I can't sufficiently stretch how essential it is that you finish the specialty investigation legitimately!

If you're something of a dynamo, you may have found numerous promising specialties. In this situation, you can pick which one to proceed with in light of the accompanying criteria:

On the chance that you like one significantly more than the others, go for that. Let's assume you simply LOVE puppies, for instance, but the prospect of detox abstaining from food makes you wiped out — go for the puppy training specialty. The nearer your partiality with the specialty, the more probable you'll be to succeed with it.

If you like every one of them similarly or simply still can't choose, look to the one with the most items with a gravity of at least 6 in ClickBank. So if you notice that "detox diets" shows more affiliate items than "puppy preparing," and you feel about a similar level of excitement, go for "detox eats less carbs." This approach gives you more shots at advancing gainful items.

Where to Now?

Go forward and win! Utilize the ClickBank commercial center and this lesson to find an incredible specialty for you. Keep in mind that the most critical thing is to pick a specialty with bunches of high-offering items you can promote, but at the same time it's pleasant if you like the theme as well.

On the chance that this appears like an excessive amount of work, and you'd favor some "accomplished for you" research and item determination in a portion of the web's most lucrative specialties, look at AffiloJetpack. AffiloJetpack offers specialties and items that have been pre-screened and chose for their productivity.

Chapter 6

Popular Niches

There are thousands of possible niches in the modern market. Affiliate marketers need to choose the ones they will delve into and try to make money from. When choosing a niche to compete in, it will be interesting to know what niches other more experienced affiliate marketers are working with. So, here is a short list of some of the most popular niches affiliate marketers use in 2016:

Health and Fitness: In recent years, much of the American and European public has turned to healthy living. This means many people are trying to eat good food, work out a lot, and supplement their diets with correct nutrients. This is why selling products such as gym equipment, dietary supplements or workout/diet/lifestyle books and guides has become an extremely attractive way of earning money online. There are many affiliate programs and networks dedicated to healthy living and you can always simply use Amazon or eBay affiliate programs to sell thousands of products related to this particular niche. One thing to note is that this niche is currently very well covered, which means there are many affiliates competing for a slice of the cake and it will not be easy overtaking this competition to start making money any time soon.

A few examples are given below.

Testosterone Increase

Advertising Size:

The main six marked items spent roughly $55 million on promotion.

Visits to doctors for testosterone replacement therapy increased 55%, from 1.2 million in 2009 to 1.9 million in 2013. Doctor expectation to recommend has likewise expanded as an aftereffect of these visits, up 56% from 1.08 million in 2009 to 1.7 million in 2013.

Testosterone substitution has become a $1.6 billion market.

Medicines for the supplements climbed more than five-overlap to 5.3 million in 2011 from 2000.

AbbVie's Androgel may create $1.14 billion this year.

Lilly's Axiron is expected to create $168 million in 2013 deals from $24 million in 2011 when the Indianapolis-based organization presented the medication.

Demographics:

Men in their 40s are the fastest-growing demographic of testosterone clients.

33% of clients were determined to have weariness.

Almost 40% reported a sexual dysfunction.

Around half of the people recommended for "low T" medications were determined to have hypogonadism.

Maturing guys (in their 30s or older) whose testosterone levels are plunging and estrogen levels are ascending for any number of reasons.

More than 2 percent of men in their 40s and about 4 percent of men in their 60s were on testosterone treatment in 2011. Men in their 40s represent the fastest growing group of clients.

Around 40 percent of men recommended for testosterone treatment had erectile or sexual dysfunction.

(P.S. If you'd get a kick out of the chance to download a free rundown of 1,781 productive specialties, click here or the picture underneath.)

Specialty Demand

Keyword	Ave. Monthly Searches
instructions to expand testosterone levels quickly	1,000
increment testosterone	12,100
increment testosterone naturally	2,900
help testosterone	5,400
boosting testosterone	1,600

The table above demonstrates the month-to-month searches on Google for this specialty.

Consolidated, they signify more than 431,000 pursuits a month and that is excluding the large number of long tail watchwords that we haven't looked at.

This is an enormous specialty with a considerable measure of interest.

Specialty Growth and Monthly Searches

The expanding testosterone specialty is generally steady and is anticipated to increment in coming years.

While it is not as popular as it once might have been, the reality that it is currently steady implies that it is evergreen and will be a huge business for a long time.

Specialties like this are incredible for several reasons, including the way that all the examination on the specialties has as of now been done and is accessible for you; there are unlimited items at a bargain, the clients are anything but difficult to discover, and there are unlimited sources to discover movement.

Sub-Niches to Explore

- Expanding testosterone levels and Increasing testosterone sustenance

- Expanding testosterone supplements

- Expanding testosterone actually

- Expanding testosterone slim down

May Also Be Interested in:

- moxie

- sex

- propagation

- wellbeing and wellness

- prostate disease

Joint Pain

Size of Market

Market slice is $32 billion

Business - 104,366

No. of employees – 449,170

Yearly Growth 3.0%

Number of individuals who have been analyzed – 50 million

Number of knee substitutions performed because of joint pain – 454,652

Number of hip substitutions performed because of joint

pain - 232,857

Number of shoulder substitutions performed because of joint pain – 41,934

Number of other joint substitutions performed because of joint pain – 12,055

Demographics

Center customers matured 65 or more around 12.1%

55.9% Male and 52.7% female clients are married

27.6% individuals have no instructive capability

15.7% individuals are assoc. proficient and technicians

24% are in control of wholesale and retail exchange

1781 specialties [new]

Specialty Demand

Keyword	Ave. Monthly Searches
knee pain	201,000
joint agony relief	4,400
knee joint pain	9,900

joint agony causes	4,400
hip joint pain	12,100
si joint pain	22,200
thumb joint pain	5,400
joint pain	49,500

The table above demonstrates the month-to-month searches on Google for this specialty.

Consolidated, they indicate more than 6,010,000 quests a month and that is excluding the great many long tail watchwords that we haven't looked at.

This is an enormous specialty with a considerable measure of interest.

Specialty Growth and Monthly Searches

Look at the pattern of interest in the joint agony specialty. The pattern is expanding and is anticipated to increment for quite a long time to come.

This specialty was extremely well-known in couple of past years and interest is, by all accounts, returning once more.

This is because individuals have more joint agony then couple of years prior, and in the meantime they are more cognizant of avoiding joint torment.

Sub-Niches to Explore

- Joint inflammation

- Osteoarthritis

- Joint torment alleviation

- Psoriatic joint inflammation

- Joint irritation

- Sore joints

May also be interested in:

- Muscle torment

- Bone torment

- Broken bone

- Calcium supplement

- Migraine

- Heartburn

Diabetes

You most likely know somebody who has diabetes.

Furthermore, they are presumably fastidious about what they eat. In light of current circumstances, they may endure results in both the short and long term if they keep make poor nutrition decisions.

Be that as it may, similar to some other person, they need to appreciate sustenance and have the capacity to pick and look over different nourishment formulas.

That is where you come in. As a specialty advertiser, this is your chance to give this support of the millions who need it.

This $289 million dollar market is for the most part dominated by North America, trailed by Europe and Asia.

With a truly large number of diabetics all around the globe, you ought to consider this evergreen specialty that isn't going anyplace soon, and venture in with an arrangement.

Advertising Size

The general size of the diabetic bundled sustenance advertising came to $282.9 million in 2009 (source).

Decreased/no sugar carbonates is the top offering classification in 2010.

Number of youth populace and kids determined to have adolescent diabetes is likewise ascending because of the absence of appropriate solid eating regimen and physical activity.

North America ruled the diabetic sustenance market comprehensively in 2013, trailed by Europe and Asia Pacific.

Demographics

1 million individuals have diabetes in the U.S.

86 million are in the early phases of diabetes.

245 billion goes for therapeutic expenses.

8 million Americans aged 65 and older have diabetes.

86 million Americans aged 20 and older have prediabetes.

American Indians have the highest rate of diabetes by race with 15.9%.

Specialty Demand

Keyword	Ave. Monthly Searches
diabetic diet	90,500
diabetic recipes	40,500
diabetic desserts	8,100

diabetic cake recipes	4,400
diabetic treat recipes	4,400
simple diabetic recipes	1,900

The table above demonstrates the month-to-month searches on Google for this specialty.

Combined, they have more than 149,800 searches a month and that is excluding the large number of long tail catchphrases that we haven't looked at. This is a tremendous specialty with a great deal of interest.

Specialty Growth and Monthly Searches

The diabetic formula specialty is declining in prevalence however is anticipated to stay pertinent for a considerable length of time to come.

While it is not as well known as it once might have been, the reality it is currently steady implies that it is evergreen and will be huge business for a long time to come.

Specialties like this are incredible for some reasons including the way that all the examination on the specialties has as of now been done and is accessible for you, there are unlimited items at a bargain, the clients are anything but difficult to discover, and there are unlimited sources to discover activity.

Sub-Niches to Explore

- Simple diabetic recipes

- Diabetic dessert recipes

- Diabetic muffin recipes

- Indian diabetic recipes

- Diabetic diet

- Diabetic desserts

- Diabetic recipes for kids

- Diabetic recipes for the elderly

- Asian diabetic recipes

- Diabetic recipes for busy people

May also be interested in:

- Low carb eat less

- Yoga

- Glucose

- Formula Books

- Work out

Nootropics

You've had the inclination some time recently. You wanted to pop a pill to transform into some genius like Einstein.

On the other hand, if you're like me, you know there's no such thing ... or is there?

Specialty advertisers, meet nootropics. Basically, nootroopics are medications, supplements, or other substances (like herbs) that upgrade the capacity of mental attributers such as imagination, memory, inspiration, and rational thinking.

So, before you bounce into this specialty believing it's another "take an enchanted pill and get to be smart," you better take a step back.

Regardless of what individuals take, without essential nourishment (i.e., genuine sustenance), nootropics are constrained to what they bring to the table.

So what's in it for you?

Nootropics are productive specialties that attract sincerely determined individuals who have the yearning to prevail in life. (Look at these other gainful specialty markets.)

Whether they are keen on expanding their potential in their occupations, to diminishing anxiety and handle weight, or just to enhance memory, they are prepared to pump their money into answers for their issues.

If you're standing there with your arms crossed thinking, "Medications are terrible for you," then I have sympathy for you.

Espresso is thought to be a nootropic.

It's even more a power hotspot for the mind as it improves sharpness, and lessens weakness.

So why not remain in this specialty as a power, be somewhat more learned than your perusers, and exploit this beneficial specialty?

Market Size

It is a piece of a $1 trillion dollar medication industry.

The US share of the above is 44.5%.

The US anticipated pharmaceutical income for 2016 stands at $371 billion.

The anticipated worldwide spending on medication is expected to be $1.4 trillion by 2020.

The development is anticipated at 10% per annum.

Demographics

A fifth of college undergraduates are taking the medication.

In spite of the fact that the correct rate is not known because it is a relative new item, the following intelligent individuals are taking this medication:

- High-level professions

- Undergrads

- Researchers

- Biohackers

7% of US college undergraduates have taken the medication at least once.

25% of undergraduates have requested information about using the medication.

30% of undergraduates confess to offering the medication to other students.

Whites are utilizing the medication 4 times more than then

next race/ethnicity

The highest percentage of those taking the medication is from families with a yearly salary of under $20,000; the next highest group is from families having a yearly wage over $75,000.

More men than women are taking the medication.

Specialty Demand

Keyword	Ave. Monthly Searches
piracetam	90500
noopept	40500
Optimind	27100
Mind Supplements	5400
Shrewd Pills	4400
best nootropic	1900
nootropic drugs	1000

The table above demonstrates the month-to-month searches on Google for this specialty.

Consolidated, they signify more than 170,000 searches a month and that is excluding the huge number of long tail catchphrases that we haven't looked at.

This is an enormous specialty with a ton of interest.

Specialty Growth and Monthly Searches

The enthusiasm for nootropics is rising continuously and is expected to rise considerably more because of an exceedingly focused market. Everyone wants an edge to succeed.

It seems as if the specialty appeared suddenly and blasted into prominence. Nootropics is a specialty that can't be disregarded and doubtlessly the interest will just increase.

Sub-Niches to Explore

- Nootropic choices

- Shrewd medications

- Mind supplements

- Intellectual improvement

- Memory amusements

- Mind work tests

- Mind works out

May also be interested in:

- Wellbeing and health

- Brain research

- Successful administration procedures

- Push administration

- Examples of overcoming adversity and motivational points

Removing Cellulite

Market Size

The market is projected to reach $12,581.9 million by 2020, at a CAGR of 10.8% from 2015 to 2020.

American women are spending about $6 billion a year attempting to exile those unattractive dimples and knots.

According to reports, the worldwide skincare gadget market is expected to increase at a 10.1% CAGR from 2012 to 2018 and will reach an estimated US$10.7 billion by 2018.

Spending on cellulite medicines was $7,712,550 in 2009.

Demographics

Around 90% of women have cellulite.

Women having cellulite treatment in 2009 — 29,534.

Women's use of aggregate cellulite medications in 2009 — 86%.

% change in cellulite medications for women, 2009 versus 2000 — 0%.

Men having cellulite treatment in 2009 — 4,744.

Men's use of aggregate cellulite medications in 2009 — 14%.

% change in cellulite medications for men, 2009 versus 2008 — -4%.

# of cellulite medications for patients ages 13-19 — 5,379.

# of cellulite medications for patients ages 20-29 — 7,420.

# of cellulite medications for patients ages 30-39 — 18,656.

# of cellulite medications done on patients ages ≥40 — 807.

CLICK HERE TO GET ACCESS TO 150+ NICHE REPORTS

Specialty Demand

Keyword	Ave. Monthly Searches
Cellulite	246,000
Cellulite treatment	18,100
Cellulite removal	6,600
Best cellulite treatment	1,900
Cellulite diet	1,300
Cellulite causes	1,000

The table above shows the month-to-month searches on Google for this specialty.

Joined, they signify more than 274,900 searches a month and that is excluding a great many long tail watchwords that we haven't looked at.

This is a gigantic specialty with a great deal of interest.

Specialty Growth and Monthly Searches

Look at the enthusiasm for the cellulite treatment specialty. It's expected to develop considerably more in coming years.

This specialty is presently extremely popular and developing and represents an ageless and possibly enormous business. This pattern will continue for a considerable length of time to come, particularly in light of the fact that this is a part of a well-being market.

Women will dependably be hunting down arrangements in this specialty, so it's dependent upon you to enter and command it.

Sub-Niches to Explore

- Cellulite treatment cost

- Cellulite treatment creams

- Best cellulite treatment

- Cellulite treatment 2015

- Cellulite diminishment treatment

- Cellulite at home

May likewise be interested in:

- Botox

- Yoga

- Mental Wellness

- Pharmaceutical

- Sex

Making Money Online: Another extremely popular niche is that for making money online niche. This encompasses all sorts of money-making programs and guides to making money from home. You could be selling subscriptions to various training courses, peddling long-term money-making schemes or referring people to such sites and earning a part of their earnings (although this is not, strictly speaking, affiliate marketing).

Here are some examples to consider.

Amazon FBA

I believe we're all mindful of Amazon and its $175 billion dollar realm. Amazon is taking a major bit of the pie, but there's no reason that we can't have a little taste.

How can we do that?

Three words: Fulfillment by Amazon.

We're demonstrating how you can rule an Amazon FBA specialty with every one of the subjects of interest, such as who your group of onlookers is, what sorts of questions they are asking, and what they are spending their cash on.

So put on your business visionary cap and figure out how

we can exploit the FBA specialty.

Market Size

There are more than 2 million outsider venders on the Amazon Marketplace around the world, creating about half of Amazon's aggregate deals.

The number of dynamic marketplace sellers utilizing the Fulfillment by Amazon benefit increased by more than 65 percent year-over-year worldwide in 2013.

In 2013, more than a billion units worldwide were requested on Amazon from Marketplace Sellers with organizations of all sizes

FBA dispatched more units worldwide amid the final quarter of 2013 than the aggregate number of FBA units joined in all of 2009 and 2010

On Cyber Monday, more than 13 million units were requested worldwide from Marketplace Sellers on Amazon

Dealers on Amazon from more than 100 unique nations around the globe satisfied requests to clients in 185 nations utilizing the FBA benefit

An Amazon 2013 study noted FBA expanded deals by more than 20% for 73% of Amazon merchants utilizing the program.

Demographics

Amazon clients' normal family unit salary is generally $89,000, contrasted with the $71,000 normal for the US all in all.

Just about 1 in 5 of Amazon's clients in the $500,000+ section claim to make a buy on Amazon once per week or more.

While 71% of grown-ups who have purchased from Amazon in the previous 12 months get a kick out of the chance to purchase American items and administrations, that figure declines as family salary rises, to 49% of the $500k+ segment.

Amazon clients circulation is 5%, 18%, 22%, 24%, 16% and 16% for a very long time running from under 20, 21-29, 30-39, 40-49, 50-59 and 60 or more individually.

Source: marketingcharts, businessinsider

Specialty Demand

Keyword	Ave. Monthly Searches

Amazon	185,000,000
FBA	40,500
Amazon FBA	12,100
satisfaction by Amazon	6,600
Indicating 1 to 4 of 4 passages	

The table above demonstrates the month-to-month searches on Google for this specialty.

Consolidated, they indicate more than 185 million queries a month and that is excluding a great many long tail catchphrases that we haven't looked at.

This is an enormous specialty with a ton of interest.

As should be obvious, enthusiasm for the specialty has spiked since its commencement, demonstrating an evergreen specialty.

Sub-Niches to Explore

- Amazon FBA adding machine

- Amazon FBA protection

- Amazon FBA web journals

- Amazon FBA UK/India/Japan/USA and so on

- Amazon FBA courses

- FBA ventures to achievement

- FBA program

- FBA courses

- Offering on Amazon

May likewise be interested in:

- Exchanging from home

- Internet shopping store

- Calculated arrangements

- Substitutes to Amazon FBA

Hobbies and Activities: Particular hobbies such as fishing, hunting, or tennis are niches where you will be targeting a very specific group of people who enjoy an activity and don't mind spending money on it. By making niche sites about such activities and having them rank well on Google, you will be getting visits from some really interested customers who will convert well and potentially spend thousands of dollars buying products to use in their leisure time.

Here is an example to show you what I mean:

Survivalist

Numerous individuals are currently actualizing the "survivalist" mindset. The world's uncertain condition has started another flood of "preppers" or survivalists.

Newsweek portrays them this way: "'Preppers' are what you may call survivalism's Third Wave: normal individuals with homes and occupations. However, they are progressively frightful about what the future holds — their neurosis intensified by 24-hour link news."

The magazine also states, "Although there's no logical information to follow the recent development in survivalism, there are preppers who have conjectured it's achieved a level that has not been seen for decades."

As per Yahoo Finance, survivalism has created an industry that is worth billions of dollars. Not surprising, considering that over 3.7 million Americans could be considered survivalists.

The scope of affiliate items is endless and has changed from books, sustenance, and claim to fame apparel to safe houses, weapons, and correspondence frameworks and power.

The rundown for items to offer is boundless and the item

value range is pretty much as varied.

As indicated by Yahoo Finance, "Given their numbers and their ability to burn through cash, taking into account doomsday preppers has turned into a multibillion-dollar business."

This niche is quite secure because the people who participate in it are much more than merely serious. Far from being a trend, you could call it a choice of lifestyle for quite a few and something that gives security to others.

In the event that you haven't yet understood it, the specialty being referred to is Preppers/Survivalists - a specialty for regular individuals who are get ready for all sorts of things from revolutions to potential "Doomsday" to natural disasters.

This is a niche on which people expend a heck of a lot of money regularly because they feel passionately that they need to and want to protect and secure their future.

Specialty Demand

Take a gander at each of the high-volume watchwords; this specialty is popular and hot. It's the ideal opportunity you have to cater to plenty of consumers.

TV, news, motion pictures, and web-based social networking nearby are making a boundless number of possible customers and clients and boundless item decisions.

This will amaze you.

Most Popular Content

The best-known content for this niche is shown below. You can use these pointers to generate content of your own, basically stuff on similar topics, but you can make it much more.

You can improve upon quite a bit of it easily, for example:

Change the post about "13 Everyday Items." Make it 20 items. Similarly, change the post about "36 ventures." Make it 40-plus ventures.

The content is almost guaranteed to go viral. If you can target the right people, you can get a lot of shares.

Is it Time to Join the Preppers? How to Survive the Climate-change Apocalypse – 11,529 Shares

Cool Homesteading DIY Projects for Preppers – 20, 348 Shares

13 Everyday Items for Survival - Survival Life – 9,253 Shares

36 Paracord Projects for Preppers – 9,001 Shares

LifeStraw: Embracing the Suck - Survival Life – 11,014 Shares

As should be obvious, individuals are prepared and need to share articles and tips in this specialty.

Jewelry and Clothes: If there is one thing people, or rather women, will always buy, it is apparel. You all know how many new pairs of shoes, pants, and hats your girlfriend or cousin buys per month, so why not have a cut of these billions of sales a year? The apparel market is huge and, with some creativity, you can create a website that appeals to a certain type of shopper who will buy items from a site like Amazon. What is more, women often can't help themselves when they start shopping. So why not also get a cut from the multiple purchases they make the same day on Amazon that you never even meant to sell in the first place? As I mentioned before, 40% of all Amazon affiliate commissions come from additional products being sold to your customers within the 24-hour cookie lifespan.

Gambling: A lucrative and long-term affiliate niche is getting gamblers to sign up for an online casino, sportsbook, or poker website, which can earn you revenue for years to come. While this is a fairly specialized field and one that may require some knowledge of the topic, organization of contests, leaderboards, and other methods of sales, the potential returns can be truly appealing.

Digital Products: As I mentioned earlier, some affiliate networks, such as ClickBank, focus strictly on selling digital products such as e-Books and online training programs. Such programs and products offer significantly higher affiliate commissions because there is no physical product being sold, no materials spent and no product shipping. This means their creators lose nothing by giving away more to the affiliates to incentivize them to sell the products. Selling such digital products can be very lucrative and in recent years we have seen more and more affiliates selling exactly such products with lots of success.

Electronics: Quite clearly, the 21st century is the age of technology and promoting things such as smartphones, laptops, tablets, personal computers and software to your customers may end up making you piles of money. This is if you are able to appeal to one of the various groups of people who may be lured in by such offers. Electronics and computers may be sold through a variety of affiliate programs and networks so, if you are someone who enjoys technology in general, there is no reason you should not try selling some.

Chapter 7

Best Ways to Set Up Affiliate Marketing

There are many ways to get started with affiliate marketing, but the best and most effective way is to invest and enroll oneself in high-quality courses or programs that can teach people how to do affiliate marketing in the best way. There are four basic courses that would help one to get started with affiliate marketing: Niche Profit Classroom, Niche Profit Course, Internet Business Mastery, and Chris Farrell membership. These courses will teach people about affiliate marketing and also about general Internet marketing techniques. Though interested people can learn these things by themselves, it is not highly advisable.

If people can invest money to get educated about h o w t o do things the right way, it will save them much time and will help them while undergoing failures or disappointments. The Niche Profit Classroom is one of the most popular newbie marketing courses online. It was founded in 2009. What they basically try to do is keep themselves updated with the current trends and also educate people who are taking the courses to know about those trends. The Niche Profit Classroom membership is currently at an updated version of 4.0. What's most promising about the Niche Profit Classroom is its longevity. This guarantees that the course will be around for a very long time. Their course stands out from other courses is that their website doesn't disappear a few months after it is started. The owner of this course, Adam Short who is a former employee of Yahoo is very dedicated toward the development of the course and for its betterment.

The main aim of this Niche Profit Classroom is that it helps us build an empire of profitable micro niche sites with various tools that they offer to their members. Now about the Niche Profit Course, its main advantage is that it involves Word Press which makes the job easy for the sites and also for the smooth running of the site. When a person gets enrolled in this course he gets the theme Chris uses for his Amazon sites. It is also student friendly and allows the user to ask a question or query, if they have any, under the comment section below the video. The user can even see all the questions asked by others in the comments and this option lets the user know about their doubts, too. Niche Profit Course's charge is also very reasonable when compared to every other website offering such courses. Internet Business Mastery is one of the most recently developed courses.

The whole course in split into three major sections: the freedom formula, the freedom business blueprint, and the academy 101. Each of these sections is further split down into more sections and learners usually start this course with the freedom formula. This course particularly tests learners about how, where, and why they'd like to live their life. These questions are vital, according to the course, because if learners are not going to have any aim about what they want to achieve, then there's no value in attending this course. This site, Internet Business Mastery Academy, is highly recommended for beginners.

The Chris Farrell membership was created mainly for people who are interested in building their own business profile and want to profit from it. Chris, the founder of this course, is a respected and successful Internet marketer in the industry. Chris has very unique techniques and members of this course are very fond of him. The membership teaches people about the fundamentals and some advanced strategies about how to carry a successful online market.

Unlike many other online course owners, Chris is very transparent and lets people know about his formulas and techniques. It can highly support and help young people who are looking for an active community. It helps people who want to learn through video tutorials and also in traffic-free techniques. People who are new and are struggling to make their ideas work can take this up. With the online courses there also comes some investment in software and affiliate marketing as well as in tools. There are a few lists of resources that can help one to set up a blog and start making money.

GoDaddy, the world's leading service provider is the Number 1 in registering a domain name. BlueHost is one of the most popular service providers that is easy to use and also provides a one-click automatic WordPress installation. It is also well known for its service to the customers. WordPress is a free blogging platform that is absolutely customizable and has a wonderful support system. A service provider can become the best when it has the tool for keyword research and Market Samurai can help discover what website is best to get into and this service provider does all the research that can make one successful. Unique Article Wizard is one of the best article submission and marketing services that creates links back to the blog and helps to increase the search engine ranking.

Chapter 8

Choosing the Affiliate Programs

When planning to start an affiliate business, a very crucial part of the early preparation will be finding the right affiliate programs or networks to join. The Internet is crawling with various affiliate programs and it will be up to you which way you go. You may choose to promote a single affiliate program or join an established affiliate network.

Specific affiliate programs can often give great rewards to affiliates looking to promote a single product or service or a set of products or services from a particular company. However, most affiliates choose to join networks, as it can be hard to keep track of individual programs and often difficult to make significant income selling products from just a single company.

Affiliate networks, on the other hand, offer a wide range of products or services within a given niche that an affiliate can choose from and start selling immediately.

The network serves as an intermediary and usually takes a small commission for its services, but it can be well worth it. Using a network can save hundreds of hours of labor that would be better spent contacting different companies, getting links to products, and keeping track of clicks, visits, sales, and other statistics.

Choosing between various possible programs and networks will be one of the determining factors for your affiliate business. While many people are drawn to the huge affiliate programs out there, the fact is that such programs will already have thousands of affiliates selling their stuff. This makes the competition fierce and it may be very difficult to beat your competitors to sales and profits.

Choosing smaller affiliate programs, on the other, may prove to be the jackpot. Finding affiliate programs that don't have too many people involved will mean less competition on search engines for the given keywords and, with fewer affiliates selling the products, it may be much easier to get ahead. An important thing to note here is that many small affiliate programs are a hoax, selling subpar products, and it is important to learn what it is you will be selling before just blindly jumping into it.

A great thing about affiliate programs is that you can join

many of them. If you have the nerves and time to go through many programs and use them for a while, monitoring your success, you will eventually have a portfolio of solid programs that have great customer service and provide good products to end users. Once you have this, you can simply keep promoting these programs, gradually adding new ones as good new programs pop up.

Of course, the reality is, as a new affiliate, you will most likely be going for an affiliate network and there is nothing wrong with this. Using a big reliable network will mean you can pick from many products to sell, easily get links, and start promoting various products within a very short time of joining. That will save the time you probably need to do grunt work, such as creating landing pages and testing marketing strategies.

Most important, make sure you stay away from dodgy affiliate schemes, programs and networks. While there are networks and programs out there offering very large commissions and great deals to affiliates, you will want to make very detailed searches and find out whether a particular program has a good history with users. If a search for an affiliate program brings up various threads about it being a scam or not paying affiliates, you will do best to steer well clear.

Chapter 9

Available Networks

As I already mentioned, most new affiliate marketers will do best to pick an existing affiliate network and join it to start selling products from a huge list of products. Picking particular affiliate programs may be a great idea for the more experienced and already established affiliates but, if you are new to the business, the place to start is with an affiliate network. There are many affiliate networks and many of them allow you to sell products from some of the world's largest sales sites, giving you an extraordinarily long list of products you can start selling right away. I will list examples of some of the most used and best overall affiliate networks to give you a general idea of the kinds of networks that are available in today's market.

Amazon Associates: As the name suggests, this affiliate network allows you to sell products directly from one of the world's biggest online marketplaces, Amazon. Joining the Amazon Associates will allow you to gain instant access to millions of products and earn commissions when your customers jump onto Amazon through your links and purchase products. Amazon Associates is one of the biggest affiliate networks in the world oriented mostly toward the American market. With Amazon Associates, you can make up to 10% of the sales price, depending on the kind of product you sell, and having a large number of monthly sales will give you higher commissions.

eBay Partner Network: Another fantastic online retailer with an available affiliate network is eBay. The eBay affiliate network is much less popular than Amazon among the affiliates but this may be the precise reason to jump into it instead of the Amazon Associates Program. The process eBay uses to determine what they pay affiliates is quite complex and more advanced than that of many other affiliate networks. So, if you want a simplistic approach, it may not be for you. eBay Partner Network does however, provide state of the art stats and sales numbers tracking, so it will be up to you to determine if you like it or not.

ClickBank: ClickBank is a huge affiliate network that allows affiliates to choose from thousands of digital information products to sell. The products include the likes of self-help programs and online money-making schemes. Many of the programs are truly great and worth the money to the end customers. On the other hand, ClickBank does also get spammed with fake programs, schemes, and books. As an affiliate, you will need to choose which products you sell and what kind of an affiliate you want to be. Again, offering honest reviews of different products on your website, including the bad products, and giving your customers alternatives will help you build trust with them and give you future sales.

FlexOffers: Another powerful and huge affiliate network, which includes over 5000 advertisers from all sorts of industries, is FlexOffers. FlexOffers was named one of the top 20 affiliate networks in 2015 and is one of the best places to go if you are looking to get into affiliate marketing.

Specialized Networks: If you have made a firm choice of a single niche and plan to stick to it, you will often be able to find an affiliate network designed specifically for your niche. If this is the case, you may want to join this network as it will often provide higher commissions on product sales, more detailed stats for the niche, and possibly better support for marketers within the niche. Using specialized affiliate networks is something that I certainly do recommend but, as with particular affiliate programs, this may be something best left to the more experienced marketers, and simply using the Amazon or eBay affiliate networks to start with is undoubtedly one of your best options.

Chapter 10

Creating the Content

Once you have chosen your niche, created your website, and decided what affiliate programs or networks you will be getting the products from, it will be time to actually start filling your website up with content. If you thought all you needed to do is generate some links and put them on your website, you are very wrong. It will take time to make your website appealing enough for people to start visiting it and even more time for people to actually use it to buy the products you recommend.

The crucial step in this process will be filling the website or websites you intend to use with quality content. There are many websites out there trying to just pass anything off as good content but, in all honesty, these websites simply aren't making any money. The ones that do make money are the ones whose owners either spend a lot of time and money finding amazing content creators, or they are good at it themselves and optimize their content in every sense possible.

Making Informative Posts

Above all else, the content on your website needs to be informative. The Internet is overflowing with websites whose only purpose is to sell stuff and Internet users, especially those who are willing to spend money have learned to see the difference. While it may have been appealing to have a simplistic website spamming loads of products to people some years ago, in today's climate, people want to see websites that actually give them information about the particular niche they are interested in. Learning to balance the sales pitches with actual useful information is the trick of the affiliate marketing trade, a trick which the best in the business have mastered.

Optimizing for Google

Once you have learned how to create good informative posts, or have found outside help to do so for you, you will need to learn how to get your posts ranking on Google, as well as other search engines such as Yahoo and Bing. Search engine optimization is a complex process that includes all sorts of steps, such as making your content relevant to the topic, using keywords and meta descriptions and tags to making sure your site is well linked up within, and getting links leading back to it from the outside.

The first thing you need to do is to make sure you use keywords that people search a lot on the Internet. There are tools on the Internet that allow you to do just this. Researching your niche for specific keywords people look for will give you the ability to know what keywords you should use in your posts to satisfy the needs of your customers. You will also want to find keywords that are not used by too many other websites but are still searched enough to give you some actual visits. This is a balancing act and you will often be walking some fine edges in choosing the right keywords.

Other aspects of search engine optimization, such as internal linking and meta descriptions, will also be very important. Google looks for websites that are well made, easy to navigate, and contain lots of informative content. This is why you will want every single post you make to have meta descriptions, meta tags, and several internal links, leading to other pages within your own website, all of which Google will recognize as ease of navigation. While these things can all be faked to some degree, the actual best tip is to keep it all genuine and have some actually relevant and well interlinked content on your website.

Using Content to Sell

Once your content is relevant and optimized for search engines, you will want to find ways to integrate your affiliate links within it. There are various methods for doing this. For one, you may simply have content that talks about your niche and is highly relevant and interesting to your target audience, making it possible to integrate the links within the posts seamlessly. This method will work well because the customer won't really know they are being sold to if the content is good enough and will click the links because they are actually curious about what the stuff is.

Second, you may use the direct sales approach. Making review posts or buyer's guides is fine, as long as you make them actually stand out from others and relevant to your customers. For instance, if you are selling bodybuilding supplements, there is no reason you should not make a supplement reviews section on your website. People will actually be Googling for these, so give them what they want. When writing reviews, do your best to be objective. While it is all right to upsell your product a little bit, saying great things about a product that is actually really poor will only cause you to lose the confidence of people reading the post. If on the other hand, you are honest about the products, people will want to return to your website for some truth and honesty about the product they are planning to buy. Instead of talking big about a bad product, admit it is horrible and provide your customer with an alternative that actually works. That will not only get the customer to trust you and like your site but you also potentially get a sale when they look at the alternative and realize it is better than the product they were looking at in the first place.

Making buyer's guide posts for your customers is another good idea. For instance, while keyword researching you may discover that people tend to look for "mountain bike under $500" a lot. Creating an informative, high-quality list of the top 10 bikes in this category will get Google to rank your post high and people who visit it will be actual customers who were looking to buy a cheap mountain bike. With some luck, the post will get you sales and make your overall domain gain some authority with Google. Within a given niche this will, in turn, help your later posts rank higher as well. Affiliate marketing is an exponential business where success builds more success in the future.

Update Regularly

One of the things that make great sites great is the fact they have lots of content and update it regularly. For starters, the more posts you have and the richer they are in content, the better chance there is you will actually hit the top spots on Google some of the keywords. What is more, Google likes the sites that update and refresh regularly, so adding content daily will give you a better chance for all your pages to rank well. Making blogs with 20-30 posts and letting them sit there can work in theory, but making a website with regular relevant updates will certainly make your site stand out more, get more traffic, and, in the long run, generate much more revenue per hour spent making or dollar invested in it.

Link Placement

Now that you are building lots of quality content regularly, you need to place your affiliate links within the content to get people buying the products. The best methods of doing so will depend on the type of a site you want to have. If you are doing a strictly sales site with reviews of the products in your niche, then it is quite simple. You can link the names of the products to Amazon or other sites you use for sales, add clickable images within the articles that also lead to the product buy page and set up special call- to- action buttons or text that will entice people to buy the product.

If your content is more general or "quality" content, meaning it gives people more than just an idea of what to buy, then your marketing will usually need to be subtler. You could be talking about a general topic and name a few products that can be helpful with a particular problem within that topic. In addition, setting images that link to Amazon on the sides of the content, above or below the content, or within the body of the content, can also lead to direct and indirect sales.

You will also send out mailers with the links to your products. You will want these products to be things that people want to buy and you will want to focus on new products that they possibly don't already own. Sending a weekly mailer to your list can drive sales, especially during holiday times and other shopping periods. Also, if you are not too strict on targeting one single niche you may want to sell to your customers based on the period of the year. If the summer is coming up, sell them beach gear, if it's holiday season, sell them Santa outfits. Basically, give your customers a choice among the things they want to buy, and don't push them into buying things they don't want or need.

Chapter 11

Converting Your Customers

When it comes to affiliate marketing, converting of customers is key. Let's say you have created some awesome content and optimized it to perfection and you are getting visitors to come to your site or blog. Still, if your only method of making money is the affiliate program, visitors don't necessarily mean money because, if your site is not also optimized for conversion, not too many sales will happen.

There are various ways of converting visitors into spending customers. For one, you will want your reviews and tips to sound honest and useful. If a reader believes they are reading a useful and honest review of a product, they will be more likely to buy it. On the other hand, if they are clearly looking at a sales pitch, they may very well skip buying the product or, what is even worse, they may look for other reviews, and click the links from those reviews, which make them feel secure about purchasing the product.

I often come across articles that use very few links. For instance, there may be only a single link to the product in a product review article and this is clearly not good. You will want to link up the product name to the sales page every time. You also want to link the product image to the product sales page, and finally, you will want to have a powerful call to action. This is usually seen at the bottom of the review, but sometimes also as a big flashing button at the top. After all, the buyer may already know they want to buy the product and only came across your site to do some additional reading before actually doing it. You want to make it easy for them to purchase the product via your links.

Choosing the right products to promote will also be a big part of customer conversion. No matter how well you write a review on a product, if the product in question is simply not that appealing, you will hardly make any money off it. For instance, if you are promoting a product whose Amazon ratings are horrible and you manage to talk it up enough to get people to click the links, you will often end up not actually making a sale once people enter Amazon and see the bad ratings and comments. What is worse, selling a product like this may also cause the visitor to completely lose any confidence that what you are selling is genuine and that you are being an honest reviewer. Rather, they will end up seeing you as a ruthless sales person who only cares about selling products, and people generally don't appreciate that.

Ultimately, you will also want to sell products that give you a decent return. Some items, on Amazon for instance, only award 1% of the overall price to the marketer. This means you will need to sell $1000 worth of the product to earn just $10. This is kind of low by any standard. Instead, you should usually shoot for products that award 5% or more, where you can actually make some good money. In the end, you should really think about how to convert every visit into the maximum amount of money, and all the above elements will play a big part in that.

Chapter 12

How to Use Search Engines

to Your Advantage

After getting your website up and running, the first thing you need to do is start marketing it online. Creating an attractive and user-friendly website will not get you anyplace if you are not marketing it. You have to give yourself options on how to set up the platform for advertising your website. Thousands of perfectly designed websites offer different services and sell a variety of products in the same market. But the biggest problem that all these websites face is the fact that most of them are invisible to the customer. This is because search engines like Google and Bing are dominant. When the customer wants a product or requires some service or assistance, he/she simply use these kinds of search engines instead of searching for the best solution that you may have. Your website will be ranked by the way you design and present it but the way you advertise it will determine the number of customers you are going to get. The only chance that your website will get noticed without advertising will be by someone searching for your website specifically by the name or URL when online. But possibility is that your portal may not even be noticed.

The effectiveness of the online advertising is not recognized by most entrepreneurs, which affects their basic idea of making their business get officially online. The process of online advertising is as easy as it can get when you register your website with a search engine that will help you get customers' attention. If the search engine you have registered with already has a good crowd, then your job is almost done. The best reason is that when a person uses that search engine to search for something that may be closely related to your product or exactly something you provide, your domain will show up in the results and you will have gained a potential customer. It is also the best of choices to go for the search engine that expects pay. This is because when you try to register with free engines, you are joining a long spam list by adding your email address and you will never know for sure if your site gets any recognition. When registered with engines that require pay, you are assured that your websites are given top priority. There are options where you will only have to pay for every customer who enters your website through that search engine portal.

The next step in advertising your website using search engines is to track the ranking of your site with each search engine that you have paid. You should check whether your website pops up when a search has been done with specific key words. Also check on whether your site ranks in the top 10 or lower. If the rank seems to be lower than that, you must seriously consider other options and the possibility of rebuilding your advertising strategy. An average individual scrolls down no more than 1.8 pages before making a decision or giving up. If you find that your website is not within those limits, then you need to move forward improve the site's ratings to make sure that your online office does not meet its end.

To create a popular and growing site with search engines that will directly show results in your business, you need to follow a few tips. You can also hire a professional consultant who could help you with managing your site's development with search engine advertisements, which can be a difficult task to most entrepreneurs. But this can only be possible with money. But many of the startups will not be ready to spend that much money on something that they might not recognize as being worth it. Even people who have been running their businesses just on the street have started creating sites to advertise their companies. They are also not ready to take any steps in building their sites if it requires money. Using these instructions, you will not require a lot of money to manage your site and also you can improve a currently well-built and advertised site.

Catchy Names

Give your domain a descriptive name. The website's theme and nature should be the shaping factors of your domain's name to make it more relevant to the search engines. If the name is catchy but also simple, it will become easy for the customers to reach out and find what they want. Make sure that you have registered your names with the top rankers, —such as MSN, BING, ASK, Yahoo, Google, etc. These are the most commonly used search engines. This might be a bit more expensive than what you imagined, but it will be effective. You should register only after thoroughly going through their guidelines. Since you have gone virtual, you may think that it is not really necessary to do online networking anymore. But good networking is the key to successful business of any kind. Just keep expanding the popularity of your website by any measures necessary. You can start by simply gaining inbound links to your official website. Spread information about your domain to other sites by giving them a link to it. As a favor to those sites you can add links back to your own sites, pay them, or reward them in any way they like.

Pay Per Click

Pay per click is the trendy way of advertising one's website through other sites. Most of the websites that are highly ranked in their own category have built their base strongly by using this method of advertising. This system uses the model of Internet advertising by directing customers of other websites to your site by paying the owner of the other website. You will have to pay every time the link on the other website is clicked on. Knowing the format for the text advertisements is of absolute importance before using any advertisements of this kind. The same manner cannot be used to create text advertisements in different search engines. Even search engines like Yahoo and Google use different formats for this kind of advertising. Go for the search engine that would suit you most by understanding each and every required search engine's rule. The advertisement's headline should concentrate more on what you are trying to provide to a customer. With only a limited amount of character space, the headline of your advertisement is the most important part. If you simply use it to list the name of your business, the customer will have a hard time making sense out of it. The name of your business can be used in the domain or in the URL and the headline space can be used to express something more critical. While working out the search engine advertisement, make sure that you are using the proper format. If you try using too many capital letters, it will only make you look crazy and you could possibly scare away your customers, besides losing credibility. By using abbreviations, you might possibly lose some customers. Mostly you should try and use short forms like "DIY," which stands for "Do It Yourself." But the world doesn't necessarily need to know just the same. Using similar popular abbreviations might help but is not recommended.

Identifying and Implementing Key Words

Key target words, which are known as key words, play a major role in helping your website reach the customer and vice versa. The advertisement must be updated with key words to create a bridge between the site and customers. In this modern era of technology, where laptops and personal computers are becoming outdated by mobile phones, making your website supportive of phones is almost compulsory. Just see that your website supports both computers and mobile phones. Including a review system on your site may come in handy, as people nowadays look for more recommended and highly reviewed sites to make sure that they are going in the right direction. Providing local address and contact information will ensure that it is easy for the customers within your region to get in touch. Even if you have established international contacts and customers, it is a good thing to establish a name for yourself in your local area. Google's local page should be claimed in order to obtain visibility in Google's maps and results on local search. You can provide a lot of basic information, such as your time zone, phone number, etc.

Chapter 13

Using Content Posting Websites

In order to make money from affiliate marketing, you don't necessarily have to have a website of your own. In fact, when you are just starting out, it may actually be a great idea to use a content hosting website like HubPages in order to test the waters. By doing that, you can see what works and what doesn't while not spending the extra time and effort it takes to create an appealing website.

What is more, such hosting websites usually rank really well on Google because they have so much quality content posted all the time. This gives your content a much better chance of getting into the top Google searches for the given keywords, meaning you will be more likely to attract more visitors and actually make sales, which might not happen when you post the content on your own fledgling website.

My suggestion when starting out is to combine the two.

Since you own the content there is no reason at all you could not post it on multiple websites and hope that Google ranks one of them well. Such websites have a lot of regular visitors and it would not be unusual to have people come across your content with your affiliate links inside by chance while browsing the website.

There are quite a few websites that will let you post your content. Some of these sites let you make really rich content with full formatting, including images, videos, social posts and all the other stuff you may have on your personal website, and sometimes even more. Others allow for less formatting but will still let your content get ranked well on Google, which is the thing that matters the most in the end.

Here are some of the most popular sites where you can post your content for free and share in the profits your articles make or that can help you improve as an affiliate marketer in other ways:

HubPages: I already mentioned HubPages earlier, but making Hubs on HubPages is one of the things many affiliate marketers started their careers with. Articles posted on HubPages can be embedded with Amazon or eBay affiliate program links, HubPages affiliate program links, or Google AdSense ads, all of which will earn you a profit and you can get paid through PayPal once you make a sufficient amount of money.

Epinions: Epinions is a review site where you can post your own positive or negative reviews of thousands of products across various Internet stores. If your reviews end up talking people into buying various products, you will earn a share of the profit made from the sale and, once you make enough credits, you can convert them to real money and cash out. Another neat way of making money online.

Fiverr: Fiverr is a site where you can do or get stuff done for exactly $5. While this is not the kind of site where you can post your own content, when just starting out you can have great use of Fiverr as an affiliate marketer. Whether you need articles written or want to share your own content for some cash, Fiverr is usually a place where you can stumble upon what you are looking for.

Digital Journal: A serious blogging platform, Digital Journal allows you to post your blog content and hopefully make some cash when you write an appealing post that many people read. There is a fairly rigorous sign-up process at Digital Journal and not just anyone can post there but, if you do make it into the fold, I think you will be quite happy with the results.

Bukisa: Another website where you can make money from Google AdSense attached to your content, Bukisa allows you to share your own how-to guides and make money in the process. Your written content turns into money with every new click on the ads.

Zujava: Yet another website similar to HubPages, Zujava allows the same affiliate links and Google AdSense ads to be inserted into freely hosted content and shares their profits with the writer.

As you can see, there are many websites where you can practice your affiliate marketing skills before you finally move into owning your own websites. So, it may be a good idea to jump onto these, and try creating some posts just to see how you do. If your articles start making money soon, all you need to do is make your site recognizable on Google and you can move away from such websites onto your own private website and make 100% of all the revenue your ads generate for you.

In addition, sites like Fiverr can help you find cheap content creators whose content you could start putting up to your own blog and make money from affiliate schemes without actually spending countless hours writing up every single piece of content you want to post.

Chapter 14

Other Online Tricks

One of the most popular and effective ways to do Internet marketing is through search engines. It is most popular among customers and merchants. The ease of use and the way in which the results are instantaneously accessible are what make it popular. There are many other ways to do Internet marketing.

E-Mail

The most direct way is to mail your clients. You first make a list of all your clients. Then you get their mailing addresses and send them mail about your products; discount coupons, offers, services, and other things. The main advantage of this direct method is that you can interact with your customers without any middleman. This makes the interaction direct and productive. Many advertisers misuse this idea to send junk mail and excessive mails to customers. This can irritate the customers so they dump the mail as spam. One of the ways to get around this problem is to give your customers the choice whether they want to be mailed these products, services or any other promotional items. This is called the opt-in method. When they are signing up, you give the customers the option of receiving these mails and, in every email, you give the customer the option to opt out of it. When you use this method, you can be sure that people who have subscribed are genuinely interested in your products and services.

LinkedIn

You need a strong network to advertise and get customers. It is harder to create online networks than real-life ones. This is the idea of LinkedIn; they allow you to make your network as large as you possibly can. It is a social site with a business theme. It allows you to create connections and carry out your business through your connections. LinkedIn can also be used by non-business people to show off their qualifications. This allows business owners to interact directly with the general public and gives them the opportunity to hire people. Since your competition will also be in LinkedIn, you can keep an eye on your competition and your customers. Interaction with prospective customers and employees is made easier and more direct. This interaction will increase your website's traffic, as more people will be exposed to your work and come to know about you. This allows you to create a loyal customer base on which you can build your company quickly.

YouTube

One of the most popular sites dedicated to video is YouTube. YouTube is a library of videos where you can post your advertisement as a separate video or partner up with them and make your video into an advertisement. When a YouTube video goes viral, it can pull in millions of views. On top of all that, millions of people use YouTube every day and you can be sure that at least a small fraction of those viewers will see your advertisement.

There are many rules and legal issues when it comes to YouTube advertisement. You can check with YouTube on this directly or use YouTube's search engine. Many people would have posted videos of themselves making and uploading YouTube advertisements. The most important thing is the advertisement itself. You cannot just post a 20-minute video of the product or service on YouTube. This will not be viewed and people will get bored easily.

You should keep a few things in mind when making a YouTube advertisement. If possible, you should get a celebrity to endorse your product. You should keep the advertisement to a maximum length of one minute. Any more, and the audience will be bored; any less, and there is not enough time to give the details of your product. Use slogans or titles that will grab the attention of the viewer. Use songs to make the product linger in the viewer's mind long after the advertisement is over. The slogans or titles should link your product in search engines so the customers are directed to your website. When the video is short, you should be able to give a clear and condensed message to the audience. There should be just enough information to make the audience become interested in your product, leading them to look it up.

If there is time left in the advertisement, you should also include the ways the customer can find. If possible, you should include your handles on social media sites like Facebook, Twitter, and LinkedIn. There is no need for fancy equipment to shoot the advertisement. You can take a decent advertisement with a handy cam mounted on a tripod or a very good Smartphone camera. The only big investment you will need is in editing the advertisement. If you know your way around editing software, you are lucky.

If not, then you will need to get the footage edited by some third party. The content of the footage is as important as the quality of the footage itself. There is no use in shooting high-quality footage with little or no content.

Facebook

Facebook has been the leading social network on the Internet for so many years that it is hard to imagine the Internet without it. Affiliate marketing experts understand the importance of social media, and Facebook is one of their most powerful tools.

Through its fan pages, Facebook can be an extremely powerful tool and a source of countless page visits, ad clicks and ultimately sales.

A fan page can be about anything. If what you are selling is legal and appropriate for a general audience (Facebook does not allow porn, gambling, and some other adult industries to be promoted), you will be able to set up pages and start accumulating "likes." Every time someone likes your page, they become a customer and your new posts will be shared to their timeline, which means they and their friends may eventually visit your website.

You can use various tactics for accumulating likes, from posting interesting and engaging content that people will want to share to paying for Facebook advertising for your page, which guarantees new likes in return for money. The choice comes down to how much you are willing to spend, how much engaging content you can come up with, and how creative you are. Basically, the more creative your methods, the less money you will need to spend. While the page is young, however, it will likely be a good idea to simply spend some cash and "buy" a few thousand likes to get you rolling, as you need fans in order to get your posts shared and start the snowball effect.

Once you have enough fans, you will want to start posting a mix of posts to your page. Simply filling your page with links to articles selling affiliate products may seem like a good idea but it usually won't be. For one, people tend to not share such content, which will stop the influx of new likes. Furthermore, people may get annoyed at being sold to too much and may end up unliking your page. It is important to balance things out. If you are selling fitness gear, for instance, you may want to post one sales pitch, followed by one informative video and one viral or hilarious image that people will enjoy seeing on their timeline. Once the dust has settled, you can post another sales pitch, etc. This way your fans will get value from your page and will be more likely to trust you and use your website as a place where they actually purchase stuff.

Twitter

Facebook was the only big social media platform until a few years ago, but Twitter has really made great strides in recent years and is now nearly just as relevant. This is why all major brands in the world use Twitter as a marketing tool and various celebrities have been reported as making huge sums simply for posting sponsored posts from their Twitter handles. A short 140-character message with the right message can be a powerful tool when trying to sell just about anything.

As an affiliate marketer, using Twitter to your advantage will be another powerful tool in your arsenal. As with a Facebook page, you will create a handle specifically for your affiliate business. Select a catchy handle and start making posts related to your industry. Using hashtags and tagging celebrities or product names in your posts will potentially get people talking about your page and retweeting you, hopefully attracting new followers. With time, your page will grow and your posts will get more reach, allowing new potential customers to see them, click the links and either go straight to buying the products or visit your landing pages where they can pick their products or learn about the things you are selling.

The importance of social media in the 21st century cannot be overemphasized and learning how to properly use both Facebook and Twitter are among the most important lessons in the playbook of a good affiliate marketer.

Instagram and Pinterest

Instagram and Pinterest are good social platforms for physical products that potential buyers might want to see. These platforms allow you to build audiences based on images of items that you might want to sell.

AdSwaps

I have already mentioned mailing lists as one of the best ways of getting traffic into your website; ad swaps are a way of expanding on this method. When you have built up a relevant base of email subscribers, let's say 1,000, you can start finding other affiliate marketers, possibly in the same niche but a different sub-niche, who also have mailing lists and would like to work together with you. You can send out mailers promoting their products to your list and, in turn, they can do the same for you.

This method gives you new visitors, customers, and ultimately sales, while it is completely free and easy to apply. I highly recommend finding people to swap mailers with, as this is really a great method of getting free new traffic.

Blogs

Blogging is catching up very fast as an advertising medium. There are websites dedicated to blogging and users are more willing to let you post your advertisement in their blog to get a cut of the commission. If none of the blogging sites match your requirement, then you can start your own blog and promote your product directly. When you think of teaming up with a blogging site, make sure that the posts in the site are read by many people. If the site does not bring in the desired traffic, there is no use of teaming up with such a site. It will be a waste of effort, time, and money. One of the tried and tested methods of finding a right blogger to make your product sell is to get a blogger to review the product. This gives the readers a sense of endorsement a celebrity would give to the product. If you have chosen to do your own blogging, then give links on your website so that you can also use your blog as a forum for your customers. You also have to make sure that the blog is up to date and that you exploit every opportunity that the current trends provide you.

Along with blogging, other social media such as Facebook, Twitter, and Instagram are extremely useful. They will help you to tap in to a huge number of customers who were previously out of your reach. These social media sites will help you to have a direct conversation with your customers, thus increasing your credibility. Simple actions, such as replying to a post on your Facebook wall or tweeting back to a customer who gave you a good review, will create a loyal customer base. The thing with Facebook is that the whole process is transparent; if a customer posts about your products, all of your followers will come to know of it. If the review is good, then you can be assured that the customers will be happy; but, in case of a bad review, you have to do your best to solve the customer's problems. These actions to help out a customer will increase brand loyalty and you will be able to know of any improvement that needs to be done to improve the product.

There are services that allow you to exchange your

advertisements. The websites that use those services will post your advertisements when you agree to post their advertisements on your website. This allows you to advertise free of charge, but you will have no control over the advertisements posted on your website. This can be damaging if the advertisement is not related to the product you are selling. These services are called reciprocal banner advertisement. In a similar fashion, reciprocal links allow you to exchange hyperlinks that allow you advertise your product if you are willing to advertise theirs. These symbiotic arrangements can be beneficial to both you and them only if the advertisement that they are posting has a similar context.

Podcasting

Whenever you switch on the radio, you will hear some advertisements. This is a very effective method of advertising, as more people listen to the radio while driving than those who read or watch a video. These advertisements are generally audio files that are inserted into the show while the host takes a break. A growing number of people are now making podcasts. It is similar to video content, but there is no video and people talk in the same way it is done on the radio. iTunes can give you access to millions of podcasts. SoundCloud is one of the many others that give you access to podcasts. You have to talk directly to the podcaster to make sure that your advertisement is included in their podcast. You can also ask them to review your product.

Paid Ads

Buying paid ads is rather tricky. On the one hand, they do guarantee people will see your posts and enter your website, but on the other hand they can be fairly expensive and hard to pay off from the sales you make as a result. There are two scenarios where I would say buying ads is actually a good idea. First off, if you are just starting and have made some content but need people to come visit your website and see what you are doing, then paying for some ads can be a smart decision. The thing to keep in mind is that these can only pay off in the long term if your website offers visitors something they will want to return for in the future. Otherwise, you will be paying for a single page click, a relatively high price that can hardly turn a profit for you.

The other time when I believe buying paid ads is a good idea is when your website has some fantastic piece of content. If you can produce fantastic content with killer titles that people will want to see or, more important, that they will want to share with their friends via social media, then it can surely be a good idea. For instance, you may be paying for a single click but if the person likes your post enough to share it, you could potentially be looking at dozens if not hundreds of their Facebook friends or Twitter followers clicking the link, which means you will be making more money. Basically, if you can make good sharable content that will get people interested enough to start talking about it, then you should surely invest money in promoting it as well.

Loyalty

Brand loyalty is very important to any business. Many businesses give something extra to their customers once in a while to keep them happy. This makes the customers come back to the brand again. In real life, this is much simpler: A bookstore owner can give away a nice bookmark and a food cart owner can give a few extra fries or some ketchup for free. This will make the customer smile and want to come back again. On websites, you might have seen discount sales and prizes for being the hundredth, thousandth, or even the millionth customer. These prizes will attract the customers to come back to the site to claim the prize. Many websites offer free trials as an option to allow the customer to see if they like the product before paying for the subscription. These are ways of keeping customers happy, and happy customers are loyal customers.

Chapter 15

Making Money

So we now know what an affiliate network and affiliate program is, how we can set up a website to sell products, and how we can use the social channels to get people to visit our website. Still, the one thing that may still be relatively unclear is how to make money from all this; we will explore that question in this chapter.

Affiliate Commission

Most affiliate networks and programs work the same way. They will pay you a percentage of any money they make from a sale to a customer who came to their site through your link. Most programs pay a certain fixed percentage, which can vary anywhere between 1% and 50%, depending on the type of product you are selling and the price of the product.

Since most people use Amazon Associates program as their main affiliate network, I will discuss how this program's affiliate commissions work in order to explain the general idea.

With Amazon Associates, affiliates are paid different commissions for different types of products. Selling video game console products, for instance, will earn you 1% of the price while selling a downloadable game product will earn you 10%. Although you may be tempted to just jump for the highest percentage, some of the lower percentage products are actually easier to sell, so there will be some tradeoff whichever way you choose to go. Some products, such as personal computers, will have fixed caps on commissions you can earn, which will often mean that selling the most expensive products available will not be to your advantage, but these are calculations best left for a later day.

Understanding Cookies

You may wonder what a cookie is. No, I am not talking about the delicious sweets your grandma likes to make for you, I am talking about tiny files downloaded to your computer when you visit certain websites. What cookies do is let the retailer know where the customer came from.

For instance, let's say you have an affiliate website and someone clicks a link on it, taking them to Amazon.

Amazon would have no idea where the customer came from if not for cookies. When the customer clicks your link a tiny file called cookie is downloaded to their computer allowing Amazon to know that he or she is your customer and you deserve a share of the profits. This is a neat little system that has been in place for many years and has worked for the most part without a flaw.

Amazon cookies remain on your customer's computer for exactly 24 hours. This means you will not only earn commissions from the customer buying the particular product your link led to, but any other product they purchase on Amazon within a 24- hour period. This may not seem like a major deal, as you may think people will either buy the product or not, but in fact, about 40% of total Amazon affiliate commissions are made by customers purchasing a DIFFERENT product within the 24-hour frame. Sometimes they even buy multiple additional products on top of the one they were looking into buying. This is great for marketers, of course, as it allows them to make money from purchases they were not specifically responsible for.

Other programs often have longer-lasting cookies and, with some programs, cookies will never disappear until the user decides to delete them, which for most users is pretty much never. Most people are not technologically savvy and don't really care about stuff like cookies. This means t h a t in some niches and with some affiliate programs, you can make revenue for a customer who clicked your link months ago and returned to the site due because o f an email the company sent them or for a variety of other reasons.

Revenue Share

Depending on your niche, what you are selling to your customers may not be an actual product but rather a subscription to a website or simple introduction to a company. One fantastic example of this is the online gambling niche, in which you do not sell anything to your customers except the idea of using a particular online gambling operator to play at.

In this industry, affiliates get paid on e i t h e r the cost per acquisition (CPA) or the revenue share model, each of which tries to reflect the value of the new customer. Revenue share is the more common method of payment in these programs; this pays the affiliates a certain percentage of all revenue the company makes off the customer, either lifetime or over a specified amount of time. The CPA model, on the other hand, pays the marketer a fixed amount of money for every new customer who plays real money games but does not pay further revenue in the future. Hybrid deals mix the two, paying a smaller amount for the new customer along with a small percentage of the future revenue created by the customer.

Other things you may sell based on revenue share models are subscriptions to various types of software or other online services, which will continue to pay a percentage of their revenue to the affiliate as long as the customer continues to pay the subscription.

Pay-Per-Click Affiliate Marketing

While these programs are somewhat outdated, pay-per-click affiliate programs do still exist and they offer some of the more forgotten aspects of Internet marketing to their customers.

A pay-per-click program, as the name suggests, pays the marketer every time someone clicks on their link, whether they make a purchase or not. While this method may seem appealing to a marketer, the payment per click is of course significantly lower than payment per sale and at the end of the day most marketers will end up making the same or less money with such programs. Focusing on the more standard affiliate commission model, is likely the smarter idea while trying to optimize your conversion and number of sales by producing great content and powerful call-to-action links.

Be Persistent

Success in the world of affiliate marketing certainly does not come overnight. While you may eventually end up building an affiliate empire that will bring you a steady stream of income month after month, the first months may be very tough. It is completely normal for new affiliate marketers to be several months into the project before showing any profit and any profits you make early on will be small. Take the little wins and keep going. The success will come but it will also take time, dedication, and hard work, so don't rush things or expect anything huge to happen when you first start out. Instead, keep learning and improving in all aspects of the trade from content creation and link placing, to traffic sourcing and monetization. The more work you put into it, the faster the money will start flowing in, so keep that in mind and let future profits be your driving force today.

Chapter 16

Myths about Affiliate Marketing

Affiliate marketing is very successful and that's why many aspiring moneymakers are into it. However, there are a few myths about affiliate marketing that should be cleared up. Among the opposing points or factors that keep someone from getting into the affiliate marketing field are the prevalent myths.

Affiliate Marketing Is a Scam

One of the very popular myths is that it's not very easy to get involved with affiliate marketing. Affiliate marketing is something where people can achieve success very easily if they have a clear picture of what they are doing or what they intend to achieve. They just have to know how things work and that doesn't cost them any money or require a lot of experience. They are just expected to have a real thirst for learning things and for achieving success.

Affiliate Websites Don't Require Much Management

From the overview, it may seem like a very simple concept but the truth is that it is not as easy as creating an ordinary website. It's possible for anyone to create a website but it takes some talent to design an affiliate marketing website. They have to keep on updating banners and links, if they don't update these things, Google will penalize them and eventually bring their business to an end. One needs to keep on updating quality content and should keep on making changes to improve it in order to be more successful, which takes a lot of management.

Always Opt for High-Profit Niches

Another popular myth is that people should always opt for niches that offer high profits. Many people believe this myth because they feel that's how you make more money. There is no guarantee that buying a niche will always give you profit. It can be profitable for some, but that doesn't mean you will profit. You will really have to understand and analyze a niche before being able to make anything from it. The truth is that one is going to gain more success only if they choose and pick the niches that they are comfortable with.

A Single Affiliate Program Is Good for Life

Another myth goes like this: You will need only one good affiliate program to be successful. The myth is that companies are looking to get involved in affiliate marketing programs and that happens quite often. They feel that the affiliate program will help them increase their profit. Maybe joining in affiliate programs could work, but one has to remember that people are going to compare your company's product with another company's product as they shop. First of all, one has to know more about affiliate marketing programs and that can be achieved only by working with a few programs that complement each other. For example, if you are a scientist, you may want to market scientific equipment as scientific services.

Affiliate Marketing Is Not Nice to Consumers

A popular myth about affiliate marketing is that consumers don't like affiliate marketing. Consumers might not have believed things like the existence of affiliate marketing ten years ago, but now it does exist and people change with the trend, so people do like affiliate marketing. Sometimes affiliate marketing may seem like an extra step and thus they would not like affiliate marketing and instead they would rather go directly to eBay and Amazon. However, it is important to realize that customers want to know more details about the product they are going to buy and they want to shop around the web. To be more precise, they don't want to try Amazon or eBay on the first try; they might even want to try your site instead. That totally depends on how creative you are and on the good quality products you put online for the customers to choose and buy.

The End is Near

Affiliate marketing will end soon, according to another popular myth. Though not cause for immediate concern, it is partially true because Google's algorithm is continuously changing. Nowadays, Google gives less value to websites that offer more links than to those that have quality content, it's clearer and cleaner to say that affiliate marketing has had better days than now. That doesn't mean that the era of affiliate marketing is coming to an end. It will definitely last for a long time to come. The fact is that affiliate marketing is still successful and Google and even the consumers know that.

Affiliate Marketing Is Not Easy

It is a very prevalent myth that affiliate marketing is very difficult. Many people who want to get into affiliate marketing think that it is very difficult but what they basically have to do is spend some time to gather all the required information about this. When they do, they will definitely realize that, with time, reliable information, and strong will power, anything can be pulled off. You might not get that instant success or your product might not have a great reach on the first day but, with time and dedication, you will definitely get there. So this particular myth about affiliate marketing is not true and we just need to focus to set things in the right direction.

Affiliate Marketing Is Child's Play

The next myth is that affiliate marketing is very simple. Basically, whatever you want to achieve in life will require some effort. Even in affiliate marketing you have to put in some effort. Without it, you can't expect any profit, especially if your website is simple without any attracting features. Just as in other aspects of life, you need to put out some effort to enjoy its benefits later on. Another myth is that affiliate marketing is the easiest way to make millions. Though it is true, the fact is that nothing comes easy. We all need to have very well planned strategies to slowly increase our net earnings but this task of making money is not as easy as it sounds.

Maybe you will not be able to earn millions but that doesn't mean that you shouldn't be positive. What you need is your complete, dedicated hard work and you can pull off anything. You will never know when lady luck is going to knock at your door. These were some popular myths about affiliate marketing. Knowing these are all just myths will help us increase our confidence and will enable us to get into this field of affiliate marketing with an aim and will help us achieve success. Affiliate marketing will always be here and growing; it is up to us to make the right decisions and tap into its potential.

You Must Work in a Big Niche

Many believe that, in order to make money from affiliate marketing, you have to pick a large niche even if you are not comfortable with it. The truth is just the opposite. There are many affiliate marketers who work in fairly small and relatively insignificant niches when looking at the big picture, yet manage to make lots of money by understanding their niche and their audience very well and relating to them on a very personal level.

If you are an expert in an industry that does not seem like a huge thing on the Internet, you may be surprised how much money there is to be made by using your expert

insights   and   professionally   made content
even with a small audience.

Chapter 17

The Jargon of Affiliate Marketing

Jargon is language used in a specific line of work. Affiliate marketing is simple by itself but you can get lost if you don't know the jargon. The following is a list of affiliate marketing words that will be helpful.

An <u>advertiser</u> is the company or person who produces the product you are marketing. The product might be an object or a service. Advertisers are also commonly known as merchants and they affiliate themselves with webmasters. The advertiser will pay money, called a commission, to the webmasters. The commission amount depends on the number of products sold. In special cases such as magazines, which require a monthly payment, there is the concept of a recurring commission. In this case, the affiliate is paid every month for the customers who are still paying for the magazine and have come through the affiliate's site. This is a benefit for the affiliate, as their income is fixed and will vary very little on a monthly basis.

The advertiser gets affiliates to promote their product. Each affiliate is paid by the number of clicks, customers, or leads the advertiser brings to the website. The affiliate, or webmaster, is the owner of the website where the product is being advertised. The URL address that sends people to the advertiser is called the affiliate link. These links are on the advertisers' websites; each advertiser has a unique link. This is needed, because the affiliate needs to know which of the links are generating income. If the same advertiser has many products to advertise, each product will get its own unique ink.

A program is used to track the number of clicks; this is called the affiliate program. This program is used by the webmaster to get paid. The affiliate program is an automatic program that gives live feed and can be accessed instantaneously. The advertisement on the affiliate's website can be a still image, an animated file, or a gif image. The advertisement can be strategically placed to get more clicks.

When you click on the advertisement and the website gets redirected to the merchant's website, it is called a click-through. This is how the webmaster gets paid. The click-through is thought to be completed when you the customer is successfully redirected to the merchant's website. The commission is the income that the affiliate gets from the clicks. The payment may depend on several parameters, including the number of clicks, the number of clicks that lead to a sale, the number of leads, or the number of visits to the merchant's site. The number of clicks is generally paid to the merchant with a conversion rate. The webmaster uses the number of clicks to convert the traffic to money. It is also used to some extent in the placement of the advertisement. The advertisements with higher conversion rates are placed higher and may even pop out of the screen, forcing you to either click through or close them. These are often larger. Meanwhile the advertisements with lower conversion rates are placed lower and are often smaller.

"Cookie" is a term we are all familiar with. It is the file that is placed on the customer's computer to identify them. The cookie will remain in the computer for at least 30 days and a maximum of 60 days. This is to track returning users, which leads to a bigger payment to the webmaster. When the merchant is affiliated with a search engine, then the customer directly accesses the merchant's website. This is called "direct linking."

"First click" denotes the source from which the user has made a successful purchase. This is where the cookies come into play. For example, suppose the customer had clicked on affiliate X to check out the product from the merchant's website yesterday and did not buy anything. Then today the same customer goes to affiliate Y and makes the purchase. Then, if the cookie of affiliate X is in the computer, affiliate X will be considered the first click and will be paid for the purchase. Affiliate Y is called the last click. Affiliate Y's payment will depend on the contract. If the contract is payment per click, then affiliate Y will be paid. Another term is raw click, which is simply the number of clicks. If the same person has clicked multiple times, each click is counted. Unique click is the click that comes from different sources. The merchant will take unique clicks, not raw clicks, into account for payment. The unique clicks are counted by using cookies and the IP address of the customer.

When the webmaster's website specialized on a particular area, it is called a niche. For example, if the affiliate is a blog on cars, then the niche is cars. It would be logical for the affiliate who is selling automobile parts or components to affiliate with such a blog, rather than with a website that is selling gardening tools. The logical match will help the affiliate to sell more products.

Those affiliates who are responsible for the major part of the income for the merchant are called "super affiliates." These affiliates constitute 5 percent of the total number of affiliates but are responsible for 90 percent of the sales.

When the advertisement is targeted at a specific audience, it is called target marketing. The merchant and the affiliate are responsible for the right marketing. If this is done right, the product sale is virtually guaranteed. As mentioned in the above example, if a merchant is selling a high-performance carburetor, it is their responsibility to make sure that the advertisement is on a website related to cars, where selling that carburetor will be most effective.

When the affiliate is given the right to sell the product on the behalf of the merchant, it is called white-labeling. This privilege is normally given to the super affiliates. When the affiliate is white-labeled, the customer will not know if they are purchasing from the merchant directly or from the affiliate. This generally does not matter, as the affiliate sells for the merchant and will be helpful in payment.

When the marketing is done properly and the product becomes popular, the marketing goes viral, all the clicks will be through a select few affiliates, and several people will be purchasing the product at any given time.

When the affiliate does any activity to generate illegal revenue, it is called affiliate fraud. There are many ways to do this; for example, there may be fake links that don't take the customer anywhere but will be counted by the system. The affiliate themselves click on the links to create revenue.

The term drop shipping is used to denote the situation when the affiliate takes the order and the merchant ships it to the customer. The affiliates may work closely with the merchant and keep track of the stock that merchant has.

Chapter 18

Managing Your Life as an Affiliate Marketer

One of the big issues for many affiliate marketers and people who work from home in general is time management. We all tend be lazy and procrastinate and, when there is no boss to answer to and no deadlines waiting, the time tends to fly by and the work tends not to get done.

If you are actually going to make it as an affiliate marketer, make no mistake, it will require many hours of hard work before you are making enough money where you can be sure you have a steady income coming in. Even then, you will always want to grow your business and, instead of working shorter days than you would at a normal job, you should actually work longer days, as you have all the comfort of your home around you and working 10-12 hours a day is something you should try to get used to. The comfort of the home with no bosses around is actually the downfall of many online workers, so I have decided to address some common issues people face when working from home and discuss some possible ways of getting rid of these issues.

The Internet

The Internet is your playground as an affiliate marketer, so there is certainly no way of not being online when you are working. But we all know how many distractions there are on the Internet nowadays. What is worse, many of these distractions such as Facebook, Twitter and YouTube will be integral parts of your work, which means you will have to be visiting them. The trick here is not to use your personal profiles much while working. You should have social pages set up for your business and really avoid spending much time chatting on Facebook with your friends or retweeting the Lol Catz on Twitter. Make sure your friends know when your working hours are and get them to respect that. While working from home does allow for some distractions, spending much time on the Internet doing random stuff will quickly eat away at your working hours and limiting the time you waste on the Internet will be one of the most important factors to keep track of. If necessary, there are even software apps you can use to limit yourself from using the websites that take away most of your time.

Say No to Real-Life Distractions

When people know you work from home, they will think that means you can always be there for them. Whether they just need someone to chill with on their day off or need your help getting stuff done, you will often end up receiving relentless calls to do stuff. You will have to learn to say no to such calls and set yourself up with some kind of working hours, otherwise the time will get away from you.

Sleep can be a big problem, as well. When you are so close to your bed, taking a nap may seem like a great idea in the middle of the day. It never really is other than if you are too exhausted to work, which should not be the case too often. Always remind yourself that your future lies on what you make as an affiliate marketer and this is now your profession, so treat it as you would any other job and do not get distracted by random things while working.

Free Days

Like anyone else, you need days off. While there are no bosses to tell you when to work or when not to, make sure you set yourself some goals. If you have had a good productive week, take the weekend completely off and have some fun with friends or take an enjoyable trip to the countryside to clear your head. It can really help put things into perspective and get you back on track to work full hours the next day. Remember to take free days and your mind and body will thank you for it.

Keep the Optimism

Affiliate marketing can be a slow business at first, so keeping a positive attitude about it and remembering that success will come if you give it enough time and effort is important if you don't want to lose motivation. Lack of motivation can be an end to your career before it has even really started, so remember to keep optimistic even when things are not going smoothly. As you know, this is something you can make money at, it just takes time. You may want to enlist friends to help you with this or join online communities of affiliate marketers where you can feed on the success stories of others while slowly building one of your own.

Organizing the Work

Keeping well organized is the secret to success in any work and affiliate marketing is no different. Especially with this line of work, there will be many different tasks to complete, from creating content, finding programs, linking your content up, optimizing your websites for search engines, sending mailers ,and all sorts of other things, it will be easy to get disorganized and lose track of what is done and what is yet to be done. Keep notes on all the tasks you need to complete and set yourself realistic daily goals to meet. Make sure you don't go to bed before your to-do list is complete for the day.

Expanding Your Business

Affiliate marketing is a business that can be easily expanded in many directions. For starters, you will usually be working alone but, as time goes on, many opportunities will arise to expand the business. The one thing that drives affiliate business is fresh content. There are many websites on the Internet where you can purchase content relatively cheap and, once you start making money with affiliate business, this is a great way to reinvest money. New content along with the old will keep making money and the profits should just keep going up and up.

Successful affiliate marketers often have dozens of websites and it can take many writers to keep it all updated. There is no reason ever to stop expanding. The limit in affiliate marketing is really only your ambition and the dedication you have for the job.

Conclusion

Affiliate marketing is a new opportunity for making money but not something to be taken for granted. Like any other job on the planet. it does have the potential to mislead a novice player and make him regret each of his decisions. Just as with the stock markets and forex, success may not always be an assured guarantee that accompanies the affiliate marketing package.

Affiliate marketing has lots of potential for those who are willing to invest the time to master the craft, accumulate a customer base, and create the content that will eventually sell products. While this is a time-consuming process, affiliate marketing is a job that can actually make you a very well-paid person without any bosses over your head or anyone telling you what to do. There are many obstacles on the way, to be sure, but the ultimate success in the world of affiliate marketing can mean financial liberty and a fun long- term job that will both pay the bills and keep you entertained at the same time.

It is my hope that after reading this book you will have a general understanding of how affiliate marketing works in principal, what niches are and how to pick the right one for yourself, how to create SEO content and how to market your content to potential customers. Following all the tips and tricks from this book should set you well on your way towards becoming a well-established and serious affiliate marketer with a bright future on the horizon for you.

The information given in this book is not only meant for enlightening you on the intricacies of the field but also to warn the novice players to make informed decisions over ad judgment calls. I hope you found this book useful and informative.

CPSIA information can be obtained
at www.ICGtesting.com
Printed in the USA
LVOW13s1106050517

533384LV00020B/609/P

9 781534 957558